For You Who Died I Must Live On...
Reflections on the March of the Living

March
OF THE LIVING

Contemporary Jewish Youth Confront the Holocaust

Edited by
Eli Rubenstein

MOSAIC PRESS
Oakville - New York - London

CANADIAN CATALOGUING IN PUBLICATION DATA

Main entry under title:

For you who died I must live on : reflections on the march of the living : contemporary Jewish youth confront the Holocaust

ISBN 0-88962-453-4 (bound) ISBN 0-88962-452-6 (pbk.)

1. Holocaust, Jewish (1939-1945) - Literary collections. 2. Jews - North America - Literary collections. 3. Youths' writings, Canadian (English).* 4. Youths' writings, American. 5. Canadian literature (English) - Jewish authors.* 6. American literature - Jewish authors. 7. Holocaust Remembrance Day - Poland. 8. Independence Day (Israel). 9. Holocaust, Jewish (1939-1945) - Influence. I. Rubenstein, Eli, 1959 -

PS8237.H64F6 1993   C810'0358   C93-095400-9   PR9194.52.H64F6 1993

Published by MOSAIC PRESS, P.O. Box 1032, Oakville, Ontario, Canada L6J 5E9. Offices and warehouse at 1252 Speers Road, Units 1&2, Oakville, Ontario, Canada L6L 5N9.

Mosaic Press acknowledges the assistance of the Canada Council and the Ontario Arts Council in support of its publishing programme.

©1993 United Israel Appeal of Canada Inc.
4600 Bathurst Street, Suite 315, Willowdale, Ontario, Canada M2R 3V3
Typeset by Aztext Electronic Publishing Limited

Printed and bound in Canada.

ISBN 0-88962-453-4   CLOTH
ISBN 0-88962-452-6   PAPER

MOSAIC PRESS: 1252 Speers Road, Units 1&2, Oakville, Ontario, Canada L6L 5N9
                        P.O. Box 1032, Oakville, Ontario L6J 5E9

American material provided from publications produced by the Central Agency for Jewish Education in Miami, Florida and by the B'nai Brith Youth Organization in Washington D.C. Film quotes and photos taken from the 1990 Canadian documentary film *March of the Living*, produced by Sid Goldberg and Howard Reitman. Photos on pages 36 and 76 ©1990 Lloyd Wolf. Photos on pages 2 and 40 ©1990 Yehoshua Ben-Or. Photos on 2nd colour page, pages 51, 71 and last page of colour ©1990 Erin Combs-Pearl. Remaining photos supplied by March of the Living participants. The film *March of the Living* is a production of the JEC of Montreal.

All proceeds to fund future March of the Living activities.

Cover Photo (Stacey Wintre): With the flag of Israel wrapped around her shoulders, 16-year-old Eve Pinchefsky of Toronto, a participant in the 1992 March of the Living, walks down the railroad tracks in Auschwitz-Birkenau, alongside thousands of students from around the world (pictured in background) marching through Poland's most infamous death camp.

Acknowledgements

The idea for the March of the Living was first conceived by Abraham Hirchson, a member of Israel's Knesset, in the early 1980s. With the help of Israeli educator Dr. Shmuel Rosenman, support for the program was enlisted in Israel and in Jewish communities in the Diaspora. The first March of the Living was held in 1988. Today it is the largest and most widely recognized international educational event for Jewish youth in the world.

The March of the Living is a program that owes its existence to the presence of a generation of Jewish teenagers who care deeply about the past, and the future, of the Jewish people. Likewise, the March would not be possible without the assistance of large numbers of volunteers who generously donate their time and effort to the recruitment, interviewing, educating and chaperoning of the thousands of Jewish students who regularly take part in this event.

The grant facilitating the publication of this book was made in recognition of these exceptional students and volunteers, whose efforts are a tribute to the memory of those who perished in the Holocaust. This volume was made possible, in part, through a generous donation given to the United Israel Appeal of Canada by Helen and Harold Shneer, and their children, of Toronto, Canada.

❖   ❖   ❖

Reflections on the March of the Living was completed with the help of many individuals too numerous to mention. Nonetheless, special thanks must be expressed to the following individuals: Rosanne & Steve Ain, Chaia Berkowitz, Barbara Blevis, Miles Bunder, Mark Charendoff, Lisa Catherine Cohen, Michael Cole, Ed Cowan, Aron Einat, Mark Feldman, Sid Goldberg, Phyllis Goldfarb, Walter Hess *of blessed memory*, Danielle Horowitz, Susan Jackson, Odie Kaplan, Sandra Kassar, Harold Lass, Jane Logan, Joel Marans, Cam and Michelle Mather, Ruth Najman, John Nebesky, Howard Pearl, Stanley Plotnick, Arna Poupko, Lawrie Raskin, Howard Reitman, Barry Rishikof, Ken Sherman, Neil Silvert, Arnie Sohinki, Randy Spiegel, Joan Stevens, Gayle Tallman, Lorne Vineberg, Betty White Strauss and Lisa Witkin. Also thank you to all the March of the Living participants who graciously supplied photos and artwork for this project. Special thanks to Ira Gluskin and Steven & Linda Schaffzin for their assistance with the first edition of this volume.

The March of the Living is coordinated by its central office in Tel Aviv, Israel, and is co-sponsored by numerous international, national, and local organizations through-out the world. In North America the program is sponsored by the United Israel Appeal of Canada, the American Zionist Youth Foundation, the Bureau of Jewish Education, B.B.Y.O. International, Zionist youth movements, Jewish Federations, and many other local organizations. Funding for the March of the Living was provided by the above-mentioned organizations, by the CRB Foundation, and by contributions from local foundations and individuals throughout North America.

Jody Guralnick
Montreal, Quebec

I think those blue jackets made us one. It showed the bond between us, that we were all here to learn about the Holocaust and we were all marching to make a statement: *Never Again.*

Miki Harrar, 16

From the Canadian documentary film
March of the Living

Contents

Hope

Introduction

The March of the Living is an educational event that brings together thousands of Jewish youth from around the world to Poland and Israel to mark two of the most significant dates in the modern Jewish calendar.

In Poland, the students' visit culminates with the "March of the Living" on Yom Hashoah, as they march together the 3-kilometre distance separating Auschwitz from Birkenau, retracing the steps that hundreds of thousands of Jews and others were forced to take on the way to their annihilation.

In Israel, participants celebrate the creation of the state of Israel on Yom Ha'atsmaut, along with thousands of teenagers from Israel and other parts of the world.

The dramatic contrast between past and present, between Poland and Israel, between the anguish of our past and the hope of our future – these are the central themes of the March of the Living. The experience provides its participants with an understanding of the inseparable connection between the history and the destiny of the Jewish people, and instils in them a strong sense of responsibility for ensuring that the conditions that led to the Holocaust never be allowed to develop again.

In May, 1993, the world commemorated the 50th Anniversary of the Warsaw Ghetto Uprising, which was led by its 23-year-old commander Mordechai Aniclewicz. The uprising, like most Jewish armed resistance to the Nazis, was organized by members of the Jewish youth movements. Jewish boys and girls as young as their early teens often played a crucial role in the struggle against the Nazis. Their remarkable heroism serves as an inspiration to all who continue to oppose tyranny and oppression.

The passion and conviction expressed by today's Jewish youth is of no less importance to the future of our people. As one young participant from Canada wrote:

> *"We must never let this happen again,*
> *or the generations to come*
> *will be marching for us."*

The urgent message of this young voice, like the rest of the voices found in this collection, certainly merits our fullest attention.

Charles R. Bronfman
Honorary President
United Israel Appeal of Canada

Philip Granovsky
Chairman of the Board
United Israel Appeal of Canada

Editor's Note

Throughout the March of the Living, participants were encouraged to express themselves in music, art, prose and poetry. The work appearing in this volume comprises only a portion of the material submitted by students from across North America who have taken part in the March of the Living since its inception in 1988. A number of small pieces written by those young Jewish heroes and heroines who perished in the Holocaust – but whose words continue to be remembered and inspire – have also been included in this collection.

The efforts contained in this edition reflect the students' struggle with the legacy of our tragic past, and with the overwhelming questions posed by the Holocaust. On the other hand, also present in this work is a passionate commitment to the future – of the State of Israel, of the Jewish people and, indeed, of all humanity.

We live in a time when, less than 50 years after the last death camp was liberated, those who deny the historicity of the Holocaust are increasingly making their views known – in the media, in high schools and on college campuses. We live in a world beset by indifference and rife with ignorance, where, according to a recent survey, close to forty percent of the adult American population and over fifty percent of American high school students either "don't know" or are unable to define what is meant by the term "Holocaust."

In times like the present, we must indeed be thankful for the efforts of these young Jewish boys and girls, whose dedication to preserving the memory of the unparalleled tragedy that befell our people is eloquently attested to in the pages that follow.

Eli Rubenstein
Editor

Preface

Poland and Israel: One, the anguish of our past; the other, the hope of our future. The March of the Living was a study in these contrasts. But even in Poland, we were beset by contradictory emotions. Standing in Auschwitz under the infamous cast iron sign proclaiming "Arbeit Macht Frei" (Work will set you free), we thought of the tremendous suffering that issued forth from the very place where we now found ourselves. And we asked, "In the face of this slaughter of so many innocent lives, is there any point in striving to be a decent human being?" All of Auschwitz seemed to proclaim: there is no judge, there is no justice, there is no plan, all is meaningless. And yet, moments later we found ourselves asserting the opposite, insisting that Hitler had failed, that life was meaningful, and we marched out of Auschwitz with the conviction that it is our duty to re-humanize the world, to restore it in God's image and not Hitler's.

During the "March" itself, again conflicting emotions rose up in us. On the one hand we knew we were marching through the site of the greatest tragedy that has ever befallen the Jewish people, and we despaired in the knowledge that the past could never be altered, that we were walking out of Auschwitz when so many before us could not. On the other hand, we felt a surge of pride in knowing that the memory of those who perished would still live on with us. And when our steps faltered, the spirit of those who died in the camps moved us onward, as we promised the past, never to forget, as we promised ourselves – "Never Again".

Majdanek was the scene of our most difficult and emotional journey. The camp was stark and relatively untouched – someone said it looked like it could be restored to its former operation in a matter of minutes. The barracks were crammed with prisoners' clothing and shoes of every size and shape, creased and cracked, hopelessly uncountable. At the end of the row of barracks, there was a mausoleum which, we discovered, sheltered tons of human ashes and bone fragments that the Nazis had gathered together to use as compost in the camps' kitchen gardens. Over 300,000 people, mostly Jews, were murdered in Majdanek, starved, shot or gassed, and then burned.

But it was not the past that forced open the gates of our tears – it was the present. The behaviour of a couple of Polish teens, who were also visiting Majdanek that day, had drawn the attention of our group. They were shouting rude remarks, and one of them actually threw himself against the barbed wire, pretending he was being electrocuted. When we reached the mausoleum, a Canadian boy who had lost much of his family in Majdanek observed the Polish teens flipping coins into the gathering of ashes. He asked them to stop. At first they ignored him, then they began to laugh, until the Canadian youth lost his composure. "My family is in those ashes," he yelled over and over again, and his anguished words echoed throughout the vast camp, striking deep in the hearts of all who were there. The brief scuffle that followed lasted for only a matter of seconds – but the agony it unleashed seemed never to end. It was as if all the tears the children had kept inside themselves since the start of the trip, were released at that moment as hundreds of teenagers spread throughout the camp began to sob uncontrollably. Majdanek, the shoes, the ashes, the inscription "Our fate is a warning unto you" – and now this! Had anything really changed? Could anything ever change?

It was a black moment. Hundreds of students throughout the camp, crying uncontrollably – and then one draped himself in an Israeli flag, as if he was putting on a *Tallit*. He spread the flag over another boy, and then another, and soon there was a whole group gathered around the Israeli flag raising it skyward. Someone began to chant hoarsely *Ode Avinu Chai...Am Yisrael Chai* (Our Father Is Still Alive...The People of Israel Live On). Several other voices soon joined in, at first weak and tentative, then strong and defiant, until everyone was shouting the words. Majdanek, the barracks with the shoes, the grey mausoleum, were all still there, but every eye was intently fixed on the blue and white Israeli flag, rippling in the wind. We had, yet again, taken the voyage from despair to hope.

Afterward, we stood opposite the barbed wire, *davened Mincha* (recited the afternoon prayers), boarded the buses and headed back to Warsaw. One of the chaperones later said to the group that *davening* in Majdanek, opposite the barbed wire, summed up for him what it meant to be Jewish: to look straight at the barbed wire, and then to look past it, to the future. In short, he said, being Jewish means to never give up hope.

– ER

It all began one morning

during Hebrew class when my teacher asked us all to sit down and be quiet. Morah Vivi was very serious which was not like her at all. We all made our way to our desks whispering to each other about what we thought might be upsetting her. As soon as we settled down, Morah Vivi solemnly stood before my grade five class and began to speak with us about the Holocaust. We sat there as still as the leaves on a hot summer's day with no wind; mesmerized by what our knowledgeable teacher spoke about. Morah Vivi went on to tell us stories she had once been told about children and parents who were separated during the war. She spoke about the kind people who hid Jewish children, and some who even hid an entire family. She spoke briefly about the terror that swept through Europe and the nasty things that Hitler did. Then and there at ten years old I began to experience a curiosity which I had never felt before; far deeper than those of the earth, sea and sky. I wanted to meet those strong people who survived the concentration camps. I wanted to confront a camp guard and ask him: why? I wanted to go back in time and free all the prisoners and if I couldn't, then I wanted to join them in their struggle for freedom and life. There were so many things I wanted to do, but I was only ten years old.

As the years passed by my knowledge, determination and curiosity have grown with me. As I have matured, I have come to realize that many of my aspirations will never be met. I will never find myself in the presence of an S.S. soldier to be able to ask him why. I can certainly not turn back the clocks and fulfil my dreams of freeing all the imprisoned Jews. However, along with these realizations came another reality, the *March of the Living*. I am now a responsible, mature and strong willed young woman who is capable of experiencing the traumatic feelings one goes through on this trip. I can, as a participant on the *March of the Living*, fulfil my dream to be there in sound mind and body; and experience what for me will be the closest I will ever come to the answers to my questions…

The fire in which my feelings burn is forever growing stronger. This trip represents more than the sites at which millions perished. It means life, hope, dreams and the future. Being a part of this future, I wish to experience the past.

> When the wind ceases to blow,
> When the trees refuse to grow.
> When the mountains no longer touch the sky,
> And the stars do not shine bright.
> That is when the children cease to remember Kristallnacht.
>
> As the children of the future
> As the hope our mothers bore
> We must learn of the horrors past
> To prevent the world from more.

Excerpted from essay accompanying application to the March of the Living

Robyn Hochglaube, 17
Toronto, Ontario

A Handful of Sand

There is a little boy on the beach for the
first time. He picks up a handful of sand
and feels the grains falling through his
fingers. He becomes upset that they are
gone, but he notices that there are few
remaining in his hand, and that's what he
has to hold onto. This is the Jewish people.
A lot of us disappeared, but we are still
here.

Robyn Kotzker, 16
Southhampton, Pennsylvania

MEMORY

We are the future of Judaism and, with that, the bearers of Jewish memory.

Howard Liebman, 16
From the Canadian documentary film
March of the Living

Poland

Like an immaculate home left
while on vacation
with all of its institutions left intact.
The schools, synagogues and cemeteries
all long for the return of their rightful owners.
Their appearance seems somewhat unnatural, altered
to give the semblance of something else.
The new landlords want to forget and bury the past,
however we know the truth,
we are aware of the owners.
We must be the ones who will keep their memories alive
and preserve their positions of honour and dignity.
They were our families
who will never return
to this place
Poland.

David Lisbona, 20
Ottawa, Ontario

Diary Entry: April 19, 1990

We landed at 6:00 a.m. in Warsaw. There was a heavy fog covering the green grass between the runways. As we stepped off the plane, heavy, humid air blew into our faces. As the sun rose outside, we put on *t'fillin* inside. With our *kippot, tallit*, and *t'fillin* we endured may stares from the Polish citizens. A look of confusion in their eyes. "Who are they? What are they doing?" they must have thought. "What we are doing is living," is what I wanted to say – but they wouldn't have understood anyway. To the buses...when the bus stopped, we found ourselves in a park. "I thought we were going to the ghetto region?" I asked. "This is it," said our tour guide. The entire area is now parks and grass. In its place is a memorial for the Warsaw Ghetto Uprising. First there is a sewer built out of the ground. The guide later explained that Jews were stuffed into the sewer, and then lethal gas was piped in. We had only been off the plane for two hours, and the "March of the Living" had truly started. Disgust and rage on the children's faces...

What is unbelievable is the size and condition of the Jewish cemetery of Warsaw. It is 83 acres of overgrown, moldy, broken, dirty tombstones. So many familiar names – of family, of friends. Maybe some are relatives? I don't know. It is like an endless forest of graves. There is a light rain, and a chill runs through my body, or is it my soul?

Warren Levitan, 17
Montreal, Quebec

Oh, the Emptiness, the Stillness...

Vacant *shuls,* now empty shells
Whose domed ceilings reverberated
With cantors' praise of God Almighty.

An empty *Aron Kodesh* in Tykocin
A bare Bimah
A lonely chair
On which no one will ever sit.

Here is the Hebrew High School of Cracow
Halls, gymnasium and classrooms
Vacated by students and teachers
Who went out on a fire–drill
Which lasted forty–seven years.

Let me reach out and kiss
Your slanted, empty, eyesockets
Gaping from doorposts in shtetls and towns.

Where once Yeshiva's *Talmiday Hachamim* milled
And argued fine points of Halachic wisdom,
Men and women learn to dissect cadavers
And consider chemical compositions
To heal the wounded body.

Who will heal our spirits?

Menachem (Sarid) Rotstein
Montreal, Quebec

Diary Entry: April 20, 1990

Outside the synagogue there are many small houses. Jews used to live there, but no longer. You can see the marks on the doorposts from the *mezzuzot*. It is hard to imagine that 50 years ago these same streets were packed with Jews – old and young. That this same synagogue was always full, all day. What happened to these people? As young Polish children get out of school we pass by them and take pictures. They love it. Some people give change, others give them Canadian pins or flags. Then they run home with their gifts from the Jews. I wonder what their parents will say. Farther down the street we came to a facade with more Hebrew writing. It was a Jewish school from 1840. From the window above, an old woman peers from behind a curtain – more confusion. "Who are they?" We see some children lighting memorial candles at a small monument, in memory of 40 local Polish citizens who died at the hands of the Nazis. Some of us light candles with them.

Warren Levitan, 17
Montreal, Quebec

From the Umshlagplatz

Plastic trees.
We stare disbelievingly
at plastic trees.
Vaguely, we hear screams
of laughter.
Through a tunnel.
Can ice cream exist here?
In the Warsaw ghetto?
We could be anywhere.

This is where our grandparents were sent.
So we are told.
I do not feel their presence.
I am not sure of what I feel
as I look up at the sun
and the children playing in the distance.
I force myself to remember
that our history is buried, unmarked
deep beneath our feet.

Lyla Miller, 17
Toronto, Ontario

Just Like Me

Those victims of man's hatred
    were children just like me.
Those who once had normal lives
    were children just like me.
Those uprooted from their lives
Those dragged from their homes in the middle of the night
    were children just like me.
Those robbed of everything they had
    were children just like me.
Those locked behind a ghetto wall.
    were children just like me.
Those struck by pain and poverty
    were children just like me.
Those taken by starvation and disease
    were children just like me.
Those forced to brave the endless winters
    were children just like me.
Those who never saw the outside world
    were children just like me.
Those left orphaned in the streets.
    were children just like me.
Those robbed of their childhood
    were children just like me.
Those robbed of their smiles
    were children just like me.
Those who never even had a chance
    were children just like me.
Those ripped from the arms of their mothers
    were children just like me.
Those shipped in from far off lands
    were children just like me.
Those forced to stand for days on end
    were children just like me.
Those killed before their time
    were children just like me.
Those marched unwillingly to their deaths
    were children just like me.
Those stripped and shot and gassed and burnt
    were children just like me.
Those buried in pits, in unmarked graves
    were children just like me.
Those all too young to die
    were children just like me.

Those flickering lights in a cold dark world
    were children just like me.
Those silent soldiers who fought off the darkness
    were children just like me.
Those one and a half million innocent souls
    were children just like me.
Yes, those children of the Holocaust
    were children just like me.
And you, who killed my neighbours, my friends and my family
    you too, were children just like me.

Jody Kasner, 16
Toronto, Ontario

Tuesday, April 24th, 1990

The rest of the group had gone ahead to explore Tykocin. I lingered behind with a handful of others, to talk with a local man leaning against his dilapidated fence. He was an older man, with the worn hands of a farmer, and tired wrinkles around his eyes.

It was a damp morning, so I stepped carefully to avoid slipping on the rounded cobblestones. When I looked up, he was pointing to several of the houses across the narrow street. Someone translated his words, "A Jew lived there, and another in the house next door." "Were they your friends?" we asked him, but he changed the subject, pretending not to understand our Yiddish.

As he continued talking, I turned to take a picture in the direction that he had pointed. I noticed a little boy perched on the doorstep of the first in the long row of attached houses. I was not surprised to see him looking directly at us. There we were in a tiny rural village, hordes of foreigners with cameras and questions, all wearing the same blue jackets adorned with the Magen David. It makes perfect sense to me that the child would be curious.

As we looked at each other, for a brief moment, I wondered if it will ever be possible to bridge the gap between our two peoples. I raised my camera to take the picture, and as I did so, an older woman came out of the house and leaned down to the little boy. With her eyes fixed on us, she spoke to him quickly and decisively. He stood up in his place, and she guided him back into the house.

She may have been his mother, a relative or even a housekeeper, but her words certainly made a clear impression on the child. He did not look at us again. As she moved to go back into the house, she paused and turned to me standing alone in the middle of the street. Her cold stare is an impression that I cannot strike from my memory.

I can only imagine what it was that she said to the little boy. I cannot help but wonder.

Bena E. Medjuck, 16
Halifax, Nova Scotia

One Reason

I remember clearly our first day in Warsaw. The day began with various tours and visits to museums and such. Just before lunch the bus stopped at what I thought was a park. So I get off the bus and I enter the Warsaw Jewish Cemetery.

Suddenly, I realize that this wasn't going to be a picnic in the park. I was a little distraught because my stomach wanted lunch and I wasn't too psyched to visit a cemetery. A few of us walked as a group through the unkempt but ironically beautiful cemetery. There were tiny little violets, trees, grass, ferns and amongst the greenery, tombstones in no particular order. Soon I found myself in awe of the size of the place and as usual I wandered off, deeper into the cemetery. The deeper I ventured, the more disorganized it got. Tombstones lying flat left and right.

It must have been about ten minutes later that Ronnie caught up to me and reminded me of our time limit. I didn't really notice that much, I was too entranced with the place and a strange feeling lured me to press on for just awhile longer. I began to feel uneasy now and was relieved to have someone nearby. Later, when we were on the bus, I was sure that what I was about to find was no accident. I can honestly say that a certain something pushed me on.

One hundred meters later, I came to a brick wall. A huge crumbling brick wall, two feet thick and 15 feet high. I started to walk along the wall, but stopped 200 meters later when I gazed upon a shiny object. As I approached, I could see a skull, shoes and some large bones in a coffin. Ronnie wanted to walk over and investigate but I pulled him back. I began to run as fast as I could, tripping on almost everything in my way.

Out of breath, I finally reached my group. They were about to leave. I explained the situation to them but at first they did not believe me. They were all surprised. The Rabbi rounded us up and explained the importance of a proper Jewish burial. We grabbed some shovels from the shed and marched on to the coffin. I found the way back to the brick wall again and waited for the rest of the group to catch up. When we reached the farthest point that I had been, we stopped and the Rabbi said some special prayers to permit us to dig. We dug a small grave and gently placed all the bones in it. While we were covering the grave, we spotted more bones and buried them too. We did the best we could finding as many bones as possible and then said our prayers. The mood was set already on our first day, for the rest of the journey.

Excerpted from a speech given at the Vancouver Jewish Community Center, September 25, 1990.

Elai Davicioni, 15
Vancouver, British Columbia

Ruach*

A desolate *shul* in Poland,
A holy *Yom Shabbat*,
Vibrant Jewish youth tried to offer up a prayer
They searched for the glory that had once filled the sanctuary.
They heard whispers of a *Shabbat* long past.
Was it the wind drifting through the *shul*?
What did it want?
The children began to sing and then they understood,
The wind wanted to rejoice in song with youth once again.
The voices of old and new combined and rose in a mighty song.
The very heavens wept, for such a glorious *adon olam*.

Excerpted

Uri Etigson, 15
Toronto, Ontario

*Wind or Spirit

"The March of the Living made Jewish history something very real for us. I
learned about what I am, where I came from, what happened to my family and
...perhaps, about where I am going."

Ron Wald
From the film *March of the Living*

Shabbat in Poland

We did the same as
our grandfathers and grandmothers
did
on the holiest day of the week
when your best comes out of
your closet
and anything negative
that happened during the week
is put aside;
When the whole family
eats big meals and sings songs
and wakes up early in the
morning to walk to
synagogue
with "Star of David" pendants hanging from necklaces
to let everyone know that we are
Jewish.
Today is Saturday.
Today is *Shabbat*.

Michal Cracower, 16
Ottawa, Ontario

Chana Fogel

Today, at Ramah Synagogue, we met a professional *Shamos*, Chana Fogel. She must have been in her late seventies. She has a son in Israel who is training to become a Torah script calligrapher. Her husband has passed away. She has chosen to remain in Poland. Of course your question is, WHY? She still has one son in Russia, who, despite recent reforms, has not managed to emigrate. Until then, she was interpreted to say: "I will not move, no matter how lonely I grow." At this moment I made a prayer for her and promised that she would be having Pesach, next year, in Jerusalem. Chana Fogel is a short woman with round features that yell out Gelfilte Fish. She has a sense of humour as sharp as a Broadway comedienne; it was uncanny how much she reminded me of my Bubba. Needlessly to say, this Bubba's devotion to life and that which she had created resulted in an instant love affair. I was the first to hug her. Since my Yiddish is so awful, I could only say "*Geizz-gezint-a-heit.*" I suggested a picture. "But it is *Shabbos*," protested a few. I immediately felt stupid and proceeded to tuck my camera away. I figured that if I wasn't going to have something physical to save from this encounter, I would study her face for every wrinkle and try to comprehend a fraction of the experiences that had attributed to those characteristic grooves. Looking up from my camera case, I realized that she was appealing to me. Once her words were translated I understood that she wanted a picture, and was already grabbing everyone into a frame that would freeze life into a split second. I will not be back here. As the tears streamed from within me I smiled, took her hand into mine and squeezed as much life as I could into the already vital woman. There must be hundreds of Chana Fogels in Poland that live lonely and secluded lives, whose identities have been shattered by a sick epoch. I found that Chana lives for the moment. We should all live for the moment. Please make a prayer for Chana.

Tali Hyman, 16
Vancouver, British Columbia

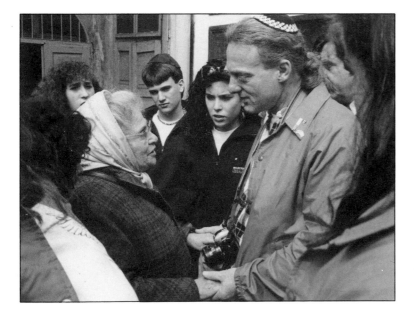

A Moment

I'm sure that for everyone on the trip, there is one moment that symbolized for them, the reason he or she had gone to Poland. The story I am about to tell is, for me, the moment when I understood why I had decided to go on this incredible trip.

We reached our destination late. We were going to Lublin to hear the final part of the Talmud before it was begun again for another seven-year cycle.

We walked into the entrance of what is now a medical school, but what used to be the finest Yeshiva in Europe. The walk is lined for about a hundred feet by dense, waist-high shrubbery, which later gives way to a huge lawn on either side. The lawn is surrounded by a yellow wrought iron fence. We walked up the two short flights of stairs and through the huge oaken doors. Inside was quite sparse, a small, empty, lobby-like place , like the landing between flights of stairs outside. Walking up the nine or ten steps we saw medical students dressed in white coats, sitting on benches. We turned left into a room already fairly full. My friend and I moved towards the front of the room where there some available seats. I sat beside a girl from Toronto, on chairs like the ones in a school auditorium with flip-up arms, only these were permanently up...The Cantor from the adult mission introduced the Chief Rabbi of Poland. He had totally white hair and a beard, big cheeks, and a warm grandfatherly smile. In his eyes you could see he was thinking of what it must have been like when the school had been a Yeshiva, brimming over with best students Europe had to offer.

One Rabbi read and explained the last line of the Talmud, and another Rabbi began the first page of the Talmud, symbolizing the never-ending cycle. Then they sang some songs in Hebrew. Finally, they began one I knew, it went "*Shema Yisroel, adoshem elokainu, adoshem echad,*" the first line of the *Shema*. The Chief Rabbi looked so happy. The look on his face almost made me cry. We all started singing and filed out the doors past the medical students who looked amused and interested. Someone later said, "I could tell they wanted to feel what we were feeling."

It was really quite an amazing feeling. Here we were in a town which has literally no Jewish population, speaking Hebrew, and singing Hebrew songs. We strolled out onto the front lawn and people began Israeli dances. Other stood around and talked. Some Poles stood outside the gates and stared at us. I didn't care though; it was good that they saw. We proved that the Jewish people are here to stay and that we won't forget the Holocaust.

That ceremony, for me, became the symbol of our need to remember the past and its traditions, because they strengthen the present and give us a future to look forward to. These are the stories we have to tell, the ones that will never allow us to forget the Holocaust and the deaths of six million of our people.

Excerpted from a speech given at a NCSY Dinner, Vancouver, May 20, 1990.

Valerie Levitt, 15
Vancouver, British Columbia

Miya Rotstein
Montreal, Quebec

Our Eyes Together

My name is Shauna. I'm 18 years old and very tiny for my age. If you look into my eyes I can easily be mistaken for a much younger person.

Fifty years ago...Her name was Shoshanna Leah. She too was 18 and very tiny. When you looked into her eyes you saw a hollow old woman.

For the last six days – here in the depths of Poland – Shoshanna has whispered her hellish story to me.

She told me of the graveyard in Warsaw where her last relative was buried alongside the outer fence – forgotten, with no one left to carry on her family's story.

She spoke timidly about the shaved off hair of her mother and grandmother that lies among the massive grey heap – behind the gates of Auschwitz.

She pointed out to me with her frail, bony fingers, the eyeglasses belonging to her brother – cracked and bloodstained.

She whispered with her tiny voice of her father's ancient *tallis* – that was once so holy and beautiful – and now hangs on a rusty hook – like an old dishtowel.

She shows me her shoe – it looks just like mine – except that it's fifty years old and tells a torturous story.

Lastly she begins to tell me of the crematorium. But she cannot finish.
She chokes on her words and tears fill our eyes.

Fifty years ago the door was shut on Shoshanna and today I walk out and leave this bloody country behind me.

Sometimes when I look in the mirror I see her pain reflected out, from my deep brown eyes. And then I remember the barbed wire of Poland.

Shauna Ullman, 18
Calgary, Alberta

Hard to Remember

Poland is the graveyard of Europe,
it seems;
but with the warmth of blues and greens
and the blossoms of *shkedim*
on Sunday morning,
it's hard to remember that
*kol d'may achicha tsoakim aylie**
and bleeds
beneath
a picnic basket in Treblinka.

The voice of your brother's blood cries out to me (Genesis 4:10).

Joshua Lesk, 17
Toronto, Ontario

ANGUISH

From where do we take the
tears to cry over them?
Who has the strength to cry
for them?

Elie Wiesel
at Auschwitz

Miya Rotstein
Montreal, Quebec

"Survivors"

"Survivors," they say
  I say "ha"
"Survivors of the Holocaust'?
  Survivors of Death, maybe
  but the Holocaust?
  No,
  No one survived the Holocaust.
  We see reminders
  train tracks, sheds, old bowls, clothes, pictures,
  books, eyes.
  We see the eyes of survivors.

> **Miriam Naylor**, 20
> North Wiltshire, Prince Edward Island

Initially, going to Poland, for me, was intended to be strictly educational. It was only the emotional aspect for which I was preparing. I expected to gain new perspective on the "Shoah". Indeed, I gained this new perspective – however, not only on the "Shoah", but on life in general. After seeing death after death after death, I learned to not only appreciate my good fortune in being healthy and alive, but that death, as sad as it is, is still a part of the cycle of life. A natural death, after a fulfilling life, is a prayer that wasn't answered for so many. How many? I lost count. The evidence I saw in Poland graphically showed me that my people had not only their lives robbed, but their right to die as humans, as well. I learned a lot about life and myself. As I continue to prioritize my life's activities since I've returned, I find my Jewish identity popping up more and more and being Jewish means respecting life and death, and remembering the slaughter.

> **Tali Hyman**, 16
> Vancouver, British Columbia

Falling

It is so hard to be coherent about Majdanek. It is still all too raw for me to worry about punctuation and sense. I have spoken many times about Poland to others and I still do not know how to speak to myself about what I saw and felt, and especially what (or rather how) I see and feel now that I am back in Toronto. Some days, it would seem as if I had never gone. Others, like today, I neglect my work to read books about the *Shoah*, to go over my pictures and to cry. Poland is still something so entirely out of my realm of reality that it is sometimes easy to dismiss. It seems that if Majdanek was real, school and society as a whole should not be. One line I read tonight stands out in my mind; it is, "It is hard to walk on earth that is so saturated with Jewish blood" and that is exactly how I feel. I don't want to write about how Poland made me more Jewish or more appreciative or more dedicated or open-minded. Poland hurt. It left me with a lot of questions and no answers. Poland isn't something you can whitewash with nice phrases and big words. It is even difficult for me to write poetry about it; in my diary I wrote that I did not want to use the shoes at Majdanek as flowerpots and I still feel that way. Nothing I could possibly write could ever have the effect of those shoes. And that is why Poland hurts. Because there really are no words for what we saw there, and we are left with the thought of Majdanek and hope that people will understand. More often than not, they don't. I remember a week after returning from the *March*, going on a field trip with my class. They were playing a war game as part of a seminar and someone on the German team said "Whoever lost, go to the gas chambers. Go to Auschwitz." I cried more then than I ever did at Auschwitz, alone by a tree at McMaster University. And people told me it was okay when it wasn't.

I think that's the hardest aspect of dealing with the *Shoah*. Because what happened wasn't okay, and there are so few words that we can use to comfort each other. Our language rings hollow and when we try to form sentences we detract from the feeling of the shoes that we caressed through the grates and from the coarseness of the soil at Treblinka as it ran through our fingers. I have given up any pretense of understanding. All that I know is this: at Majdanek, I was terrified of falling into the ashes.

Lisa Gruschcow, 15
Toronto, Ontario

From One Who Has Tasted Ashes

Long I stood
staring at the mound
numb
death is not a concept
not an event
it has a shape, mass, dimensions.

So I stood and stared
mouth agape
here is death
in this pile of bones and ashes.

It is cold
the wind blows
I cannot feel the cold
not on the outside

It happens
quite natural
wind, ashes
a strong gust
I squint my eyes
something in there
they start to tear

then
a taste of grit in my mouth

how can one swallow when one has
tasted
ashes
how can one dare to spit them out.

Anonymous
Toronto, Ontario

Me Too

Do you know how many times I have said
"Me Too?"
Do you know how many times people cried
and I cried, too?
Do you know how many times people had hope
and I did, too?
It's in all of our eyes
We share the candle
intertwined,
sadly beautiful
Havdallah:
the end and yet the beginning.
Fire can be used for bad or for good
If you see the burning flames of yesterday
In your small candle –
Walk forward and put your fire
to good use,
If you question this
Just look in my eyes,
for they say, "Me Too."

Marni Levitt, 15
Toronto, Ontario

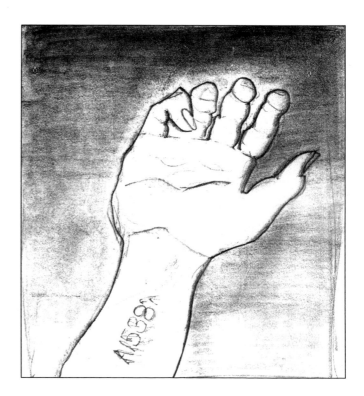

Hartley Wynberg
Toronto, Ontario

Yad (The Hand)

There is little more powerful than the touch of a hand. Sometimes a place is found where words become too frightening, and only a hand can reach beyond the boundaries to convey what mortal mouths are too numb to speak. Sometimes there are no words left to say what must be said; our souls are spent, and only a touch can warm a heart made cold by silence. A hand can comfort, soothe, nurture, guide, invite, caress, search, chastise... and repel, taunt, punish, curse, hurt, torture. For a hand can also come unwanted and with iron fingers rip apart all decency and sanity and burn the flesh beneath it until the soul cries out.

Ever since I was a child I have heard stories about one hand, the cruelest hand. It was the hand with the finger that pointed the way at Auschwitz. That finger had the power of human destiny, and sent one to death or to an impossible chance of survival. To the right, or tho the left...On a whim? An impulse? An appraisal? No one asked any questions of the hand.

I feared the hand and hated it, though I never saw it. It followed me through the years and forced its way into my thoughts. In my mind it loomed immense and terrible. There were no eyes and no ears and certainly no head. Just a hand, obese with the power that nothing on this earth should ever possess, laughing a cruel inhuman laugh as it severed dreams and hopes and families with a single motion.

I went to Auschwitz. I walked through that fearful place where death is on display in unending glass cases. I felt the hands that had been bloated by gas and devoured by flame reaching for me, imploring me to save them, but I could not grasp them and they slipped away into the fires. While their clawing fingers could still have grasped life there were no outstretched arms, and now they are forever beyond our reach.

I almost lost myself as I saw the things once cherished by living, breathing, loving people; all that is left of millions, and the pictures of their time there in hell. Their belongings now lie in careless heaps. No one loves those things now – no one is left to love them.. Blinded by pain and confusion I staggered in the darkness. But the hands of the living caught me as I stumbled and I held them as they faltered. Holding each other we walked through that place, sustaining each other with the strength that none of us had alone.

Among the endless display that line the walls of the barracks of the expanse that is Auschwitz there is a photograph. It is a picture of confusion and terror, for everything and everyone at Auschwitz was confused and terrified. It shows an enormous mass of people. And in the center, a man. A man holding out his hand. His finger points. Points the way to life or death.

It was just a hand. A human hand.

Yad (The Hand) *refers to the infamous Dr. Mengele who, with the motion of his hand, made many of the selections at Auschwitz, sending new arrivals to work or to the gas chambers.*

Ayelet Cohen, 16
Montreal, Quebec

Where Have You Gone?

Where are you little Moshe?
Where have you gone?
The last I was told, you were alone and afraid –
taken from your mother's arms – only nine years old.
The sound of her voice calling your name
consumed your ears
as they forced her into the distance – forever.

Where are you little Moshe?
Where have you gone?
I've come back here to save you, to ease your pain.
But all I've found are barren fields echoing –
empty silences.
Is it possible that you were taken too,
and that no one answered your cries?

Where are you little Moshe?
Where have you gone?
Is it true that no one heard you? –
That the ears of mankind became deafened
even to the cries of a child.
Was there anyone there, to sing you a lullaby Moshe,
when you were afraid?
I am here now.
Where are you little Moshe?

Of course, now I see you
Walking in the light.
Your father, Abraham, holding your hand.
Surely you walk before the Almighty One –
You who kept the covenant, and died for being a Jew.
Surely you walk before Him –
For your sins were none, and your tears He counted.

Joanna Raby, 17
Montreal, Quebec

A Million Years Ago, a Billion Miles Away

She lived for three long years
in that earth packed hole.
Trembling under the footsteps.
They grew louder every time.
She was just seventeen, like me.
But her world was full of pain
A million years ago, a billion miles away.

I light up a candle
for you, and those you lost.
From my heart comes a silent prayer for you.
I still remember.
We will never walk alone again
upon this blood-soaked land.
We will protect this pile of ashes
the wind can't carry them away.

We struggle to cross the line
between the present and the past.
Here we rested; now we're strangers here.
How many others walked this path?
I picked up a faded tombstone.
Couldn't read a word it said.
But to me it was yours.
A million years ago, a billion miles away.

Lyla Miller, 17
Toronto, Ontario

"One of the reasons I went on the "March" was because I felt a personal obligation to those who were murdered. On Shabbat in Warsaw, when I stood on the steps of Mila 18 and sang the partisans' song, I felt that I had, in some way, fulfilled that obligation."

Anonymous
Montreal, Quebec

We Did Not Return Unchanged

No one who journeys to the death camps in Poland returns unchanged.
No one who looks at or weeps over the ruins of the crematoria at Birkenau, the thousands of stone markers at Treblinka, the mound of human ash at Majdanek, the wall of blood at Auschwitz, ever remains unchanged.
I was a chaperone on this journey. Chaperones are supposed to lead. But I was led. And I was changed. Because the hands that clasped mine, the arms that embraced me, the tears that mingled with mine strengthened me and gave me hope in those very places where for many hope had once failed. Not this time. Not ever again. That was what I learned. And that was what the marchers learned.
We did not return unchanged.

Harold Lass
Toronto, Ontario

"At the end of the March itself we had a ceremony in Birkenau...the most touching thing for me was that at the end we placed tombstones, makeshift tombstones, for people who probably never had tombstones made for them."

Warren Levitan
From the film *March of the Living*

March of the Living: The Beauty in Hell

How can I describe to you the anger I felt seeing the
beauty in hell
the green, the flowers, the blue sky
all the nature I'd been used to seeing everyday,
but not in hell
They don't belong here, I thought
I picked up a deserted bird's home
clutching it, the dirt crumbled through by fingers
the dead, dried, decayed grass stiff.
I held it walking through hell trying to depict other life.

And when I discovered that all was left were the
terrifying shadows of death
My heart pounded and I ran out – unable to escape it
weeping from sorrow and grief,
still holding the nest,
the home of a bird I had not known.

This bird was a part of me,
I thought,
its home shouldn't be here.
not in hell.

Chaya Epstein, 15
Vancouver, British Columbia

The Girl in the Blue Jacket

Hello there
You remember me, don't you
I'm the girl in the blue jacket
Yes, that's the one
Sitting in the back of your closet
Collecting dust
We look a lot alike, don't we
I know you well and yes,
You know me too
You like parties and shopping and boys
You like to write and draw
but do your nightmares leak onto the paper
As mine sometimes do?
Time has passed
We seem to be growing farther and farther
Apart.
Don't forget me
Don't forget them
Don't think of graves or camps or numbers
Think of me
Think of who you were
And what you are
What you got there
And what you left behind
There's nothing wrong with boys and parties
Nothing wrong with living.
Life is so fragile, so short
Live on the dance floor
Not in the graveyard
But don't forget.
Because that graveyard you've forgotten is
your past
And you are empty without it

Live today
But remember the girl in the blue
jacket.
Remember me.
I am still there.
Not in that blue jacket
In the back of the closet
Collecting dust.
I am in that twinkle in your eye
When you think of Israel
And in the tear that falls
From that same eye
I am on the pages of your journal
And of your heart.
Do you see me?
I see you.
And yes, now you see too.
Remember the girl in the blue
jacket
Remember me.
Remember yourself.
Remember them.

Aviva Goldberg, 17
Winnipeg, Manitoba

Never in Eternity

I'm sorry if I didn't see your face...
>among the hundreds of shattered eyeglasses, tons of beautiful hair,
thousands of unmatched shoes, caps, shirts, or pants.

I'm sorry if I couldn't taste your bitter tears...
>as you were separated from your beloved family,
as you were tortured, beaten, or raped,
as you were forced to dig your own grave,
or stand naked, cramped together with hundreds of others
in the "shower", which you knew was really a gas chamber.

I'm sorry if I wouldn't hear your painful cries...
>At first, I wanted to experience your horror through my ears,
but as your piercing screams began to echo through the walls,
I cringed and refused to open my ears.

I'm sorry if I'll never feel the same as you did...
>The humiliation of standing naked among fellow Jews
and taunting, mocking Nazi soldiers,
Being treated worse than any animal has ever been treated,
Being robbed of every human dignity,
And being forced to face tasks more difficult
than a mule or an ox.

I will never, ever be able to comprehend the Hell
that you were forced to endure

>...Never in eternity

Elisa Frame, 17
Medford, New Jersey

The GO Bus, a Boy and a Swastika

I was on the GO Bus, on my way home from work. I was sitting in the back of the bus where two long rows of seats face each other. Across from me, I saw a boy who must have been fifteen or sixteen. He was cool, good-looking. His hair was light brown, almost blond, and it had a mushroom cut. His light eyes sparkled with vigor and youth. He was tall, and well-built for his age. (I imagine that a lot of girls think that he is cute.) He was listening to his walkman: a teenager, like the rest of us.

Like the rest of us...but not quite. There was one thing that made him different from many of the people I have known. I could not look away from him or his knapsack. On his knapsack, he had penned: "Cool rules," "Angry as U wanna be," a drawing of what looked like a little bomb. Having known guys who worshipped Rambo and Clint Eastwood, I did not think much of these. Anyhow, it was not these that made me tremble. It was the symbol engraved on the pocket of his knapsack with a bloody red pen. I could not take my eyes off of it. It was a swastika.

At that moment, I felt more intensely than I had felt on many points during our trip. My heart was beating faster than usual and my hands were shaking in shock, anger, and fright.

Of course I had seen swastikas before. One was even spray-painted on the wall of the synagogue right outside my school, not to mention all the movies and the documentaries, the neo-Nazis, skinheads, satan worshippers and the KKK. But here was a young boy who could have been my friend. He looked so innocent. I knew he was. Didn't he know what the symbol meant? Didn't he know how many people died because of it? Didn't he know of the inhumanity and absolute...horror and evil that the symbol represented?

I wanted to talk to him. I wanted to ask him if he knew what the swastika, the insignia of Nazi Germany symbolized: an ideology that killed millions of people. In my head, I had a little conversation with him:

"Do you know what that sign symbolizes?" I would hear an answer from him, probably a short one. But I would continue.

"It is the symbol of the Nazis. The people who killed thousands in the war. They put them in ovens. They burned them to death. They gassed them. They made them dig their own graves and then shot them. They shaved people's hair and used it to make clothing. Damn it, how can a guy like your decorate his bag with a swastika? Don't you know what it means?"

I had this "conversation" in my head, though. I am always hesitant to talk to people for the first time, especially if I am the one starting the conversation.

"But you've got to confront him," I told myself. "You must. Be brave..."

There were only three stops left to my destination. "Do it now or do it never," I threatened myself. Finally, with my heart beating furiously, I looked him in the eye and waved my hand to get his attention.

He looked at me and he smiled. It was a sweet smile.

I thought to myself that he probably knows a bit about the symbol. But he thinks it is cool, like the peace symbol. Hey, if the sign was not representative of so much..., I would think that it is a neat little sign too. But he just thinks the sign is cool and does not really know. He thinks the sign is cool, and doodles it all over his notes without really knowing the meaning behind it. He does this the way we all do so many things without stopping to look at the meaning behind our actions.

"Can I ask you something?" I said.

Still smiling, he held up his finger, asking me to wait while he turned off his walkman. Then he took the plugs out of his ears. He was polite.

"Why do you have the swastika on your bag?"

He shrugged his shoulders, still smiling.

"Do you know what it symbolizes?"

"Yeah. Nazi Germany." He was still smiling, his eyes sparkling. Did he think that he had impressed me with his knowledge?

"They killed a lot of people."

"Yeah, I know." His smile was a bit awkward now.

No, what I said did not sound at all the way that I wanted it to.

"They gassed people and burned them in ovens." I was talking too fast, I think. I continued, however. "I was just there, in the concentration camps, and just seeing that sign now makes me shiver."

He was not smiling anymore, but he did not look penitent either. He just nodded his head a few times and said "O.K." I knew that he must have felt uncomfortable. He said, "O.K.", and leaned back in his seat and put his earplugs back in. I was ready to get up and get off the bus. I wanted to tell him, "Hey, I just wanted you to know...That sign, it isn't anything to be shown off."

But as I got up to leave and stood above the steps, he did not look at me. He looked straight ahead stiffly. As the bus came to a stop, I patted him lightly on the shoulder, and he turned. We smiled at each other, and I got off.

I was upset that I had not really made him understand why it was wrong to put that symbol on a bag. But I did not regret, in fact I felt glad that I spoke to him.

I knew, though, that my "speech" was not enough. He had that sign on his bag because of ignorance: an ignorance that was a result of faulty education; ignorance caused by a generally unaware society; ignorance which could give way to the acceptance of those who deny the Holocaust ever happened; ignorance that could result in the repetition of history.

There are thousands of students, like the guy on the bus, who see in the swastika a symbol as innocuous as a maple leaf. And so, for the first time in my life, I felt deeply compelled to do something to keep the memory of the Holocaust alive – not because I felt that it was my responsibility to do so, but because I saw that boy and the symbol on his bag, cool and meaningless to him and the majority of our generation, but significant and full of horror to others.

Dyanoosh Youssefi, 19
Toronto, Ontario

The author, who escaped to Canada from Iran at the age of 12, had her story published in the Toronto Star, *in July 1990. It was also reprinted in* "What's Fair", *a high school text dealing with moral issues, published by Prentice-Hall.*

Auschwitz

Frozen
I could only stand and stare at the thing.
More than ugly,
More than horrific,
More than terrifying.
Surpassing the boundaries of ultimate evil to a
world I could never have dreamed existed.
Worse than in my most terrible nightmare,
Worse than anyone's worst nightmare could possibly be
So I stood
Paralysed
And could not find any words
Only to be consumed by an overwhelming feeling of
something that I still can find no words for.
And I still shiver
And cry
As I remember
And relive
The feeling
I can still smell the smoke that was in the air from
a nearby train.
I can still feel the wind rush by my body
And the moisture in the air from the cloudy sky.
And I can still close out the world around me
As the thing sits smugly, watching me watch it.
Right now there are only two things in existence:
Myself and this thing
I feel it waiting for me
Coldly sitting and waiting and laughing
And I am lost,
I am falling
And I cannot escape it
This wrenching, squirming, bursting, slithering
explosion of a feeling which defies definition
This cold fear has slapped me in the face and is
slowly seeping in through my skin.
I am repelled by and yet drawn to this monster
I have been kidnapped by this enormity of fear of
a sheer terror that is the essence of this place
A part of me is gone forever, and in it's place is the
unmistakable image of the gas chamber and the crematorium.

Don't you know what this is? My body screamed at the world.
I am incredulous as to how the planet can carry on with this thing
marring it's very being.

Anguish

I can hear the quickened pace of my breathing
I can hear my heart pounding
But the screaming is all in my mind, and in that endless plea
I hear my voice, too.
But suddenly they all stop
And only I am left
Alone
Screaming
Ashamed that I could be terrified of something that I did not have to go through.

I beg forgiveness from the dead for my trying to imagine
something I could never, never possibly imagine.

And I sing for you
I cry for you
I hope for you
And I will always fight for you
And most of all
I will teach for you
And live for you
And I remember you
I
Will always
Always
Remember

Caroline Liffman, 16
Winnipeg, Manitoba

Becky Saka
Miami, Florida

Empty

Empty is how I feel,
empty describes the barracks
ridden of evidence to their torture
empty is my heart
yearning for their lives
destroyed by hate, power, and greed.
People condemned to pay for crimes undone.
Individuals, branded as one, united in suffering,
identified by a yellow star.
A world enclosed in evil, humanity conformed and collapsing,
trapped by merciless tyrants, who displayed no human compassion.
The streets of Poland are empty, yet full of spirits.
Everywhere I look I see their holy faces.
In the sky, streets, and buildings.
They guide us through Poland, and will rejoice with us in Israel.
Their overwhelming cries echo beneath the wind.
There is a presence of peace and contentment within the evil of generations past.
Significant symbols of their pain surround our journey.
Again my imagination wanders to their sorrow filled faces that reveal smiles as we
sing songs of memorial, hope, and freedom.
The rain falls gently on our faces in formations of tears overflowing from heaven.
We march in a unison of faith, and for a brief moment the emptiness is shattered and
replaced by hope.

Shoshana Dayan, 17
Vancouver, British Columbia

It Is Done

I want to hug that person,
but all I will feel is a gravestone.
I want to return it upright,
but the stone stands crooked.
History stays put
and all I can do is remember it.

Written after a visit to the Jewish Cemetery in Warsaw

Marni Levitt, 15
Toronto, Ontario

Elie Wiesel at Auschwitz

Excerpted

"How can one not be concerned about anti–Semitism? We were convinced that anti-Semitism perished here. Anti–Semitism did not perish; its victims perished here. Children of the Jewish People, will you ever see what I see here? I see so many children and so many parents, so many teachers and so many students. I see them, forever will I see them. I see them walking in their nocturnal processions, wandering, crying, praying."

"Forever will I see the children who no longer have the strength to cry.
Forever will I see the elderly who no longer have the strength to help them.
Forever will I see the mothers and the fathers, the grandfathers and the grandmothers, the little school children...their teachers...the righteous and the pious...
From where do we take the tears to cry over them?
Who has the strength to cry for them?"

"Years and years ago – I cannot tell you what I saw – I am afraid – I am afraid that if I told you, we would all break out in tears and never stop. I see a young girl..."

At this point, Elie Wiesel shook his head and left the microphone, unable to finish the story he had begun.

Elie Wiesel, Nobel Laureate, survivor, and noted writer on the Holocaust, spoke to the thousands of March of the Living participants at the closing ceremony in Auschwitz in 1990.

Please

Don't make me talk.
Please, don't make me talk,
And don't make me see
Please, I don't want to see anymore.
My eyes have looked into their eyes.
My hands have touched pieces of their lives,
And my feet have walked on their graves.
So please don't make me talk.
Don't make me tell their story
Because all you will hear will be pain,
Pain and Anger.
Pain, Anger and Fear.
Pain of their bodies and their souls.
Anger in their minds and their spirits
But the fear, the fear is mine.
Fear of the images in my mind.
But if I do talk,
Please listen,
And please, please dear God, please remember.

Talia Klein, 17
Guelph, Ontario

Visiting the concentration camps put the events of the Holocaust in the realm of reality for me. Seeing that the place where it happened has birds, grass and trees and is inhabited by people who are fundamentally no different from us, has transformed the Holocaust from a nightmare that we share as a culture to a real event that happened to people like me. This trip made it more evident that in our world, people like me can be slaughtered en masse and be powerless to do anything about it, that people like me can stand by and watch this happen and that, most of all, people like me with education, culture and family can apply the principles of Henry Ford towards the killing of human beings rather than the building of automobiles. Surprisingly, on this trip in which I have seen the worst humanity has to offer, I feel myself more closely linked to my fellow man, whether he be a Muslim fundamentalist, a white supremacist or a New York Yankee fan. Although I find myself with the same frustration and anger for anti-Semites and racists' bigotry, I have a new found tolerance for them since I have come to the realization that these people are not the supernatural incarnation of evil on this planet, but rather ordinary people with a form of intellectual blindness. I believe answering them with hatred will only aggravate the situation, giving them justification for their beliefs.

Darryl Benjamin, 18
Toronto, Ontario

The March of the Living

Picture yourself on a field of beautiful green grass. The sun is shining. The birds are singing. The sky is as blue as ever. Many red-brick-house-like structures surround you. Where are you? You are in the middle of Auschwitz 1, a concentration camp that was the graveyard of thousands of Jews and other minorities, only five decades ago. You close your eyes and try to see the suffering prisoners and the merciless guards. But all you can see is the ironic beauty of this place...

We gave the remaining Jews of Poland tremendous hope as they saw four thousand Jews from thirty-seven different countries join together on *Yom Hashoah*, Holocaust Memorial Day. We marched, six abreast, in silence, all wearing our blue jackets, from Auschwitz 1 to Auschwitz 2 (Birkenau). There was an eery similarity between our silent march and the one that took place fifty years ago, when millions of Jews marched just as we did. Only they were not marching to life. They were marching to death, an inexplicable torturous death. In Birkenau, the remains of a crematorium destroyed by the Nazis just before liberation, served as a podium for our ceremony. Although there were tears in everyone's eyes, there was in every heart, a flame burning with hope for the future, and the strength and will to never let a tragedy like this ever happen again to anyone...

I will remember these things forever. I will remember the seas of shoes, the mounds of hair, the brushes, the eyeglasses, the pots and pans, the seven tons of human ashes, and, of course, the suitcases upon which I saw familiar names.

Never before have I been so proud to be Jewish. Whether I feel sad for the past or happy for the present, I have learned that the future will only be as good or as bad as we make it.

Excerpted from an essay

Shauna Zeilig, 15
Toronto, Ontario

Diary Excerpt: April 23, 1990

Majdanek – there is no way to describe it. There is so much death here that you can feel it creep through your skin. I could try to tell you the things that I saw there, but that would make everything a story that has passed and should be buried. But how do I explain the things I feel? I do not know the words. So, I must tell you what I saw, what I heard and how I felt, as well as I can.

I began to walk through the barracks with my friends. The wind was strong. It cried and wailed, pushing me forward. The cold stung my ears. It was April. I was thankful for my hair. It covered my face, shielding it from the cold hard blade of the persistent wind. I walked into one of the barracks with my hands in my pockets. The room was full of cages. Within these cages there were shoes. Baby shoes, working shoes, dress shoes and sandals. Every one of them smelled of old leather. It was a strong stale smell. The wind whistled through the cracks in the barracks. It was a baby's cry, a girl's cry, an old man's cry. I reached through the cages to touch the shoes and when I took my hand away I saw a layer of dust – brown dust. I walked further, saw a woman's dress shoe and reached out for it. I pulled my face towards the cage and gripped the shoes, smelled the leather and began to cry. I cried together with the children, mothers, fathers, grandmothers, and grandfathers. I cried for them and with them.

I lit a candle with the Rabbi's lighter. I left the barrack, and walked to him to return his lighter. I was about to turn back but he told me that it was all just shoes. I understood. I walked into the next barrack. There is only one way I can explain it. Imagine: You are at the sea. You walk from the land out onto a dock. You keep walking for a distance of 90 feet. Now, turn around and look at the water. Do you see it rippling in the wind? Do you smell the salt? Now look again. The water has turned into piles of dirty leather shoes. One on top of the other, hundreds on top of hundreds. All tired from hard wear, their soles worn out and many times completely gone. A sea of shoes.

Tell me, how do you feel?

I'll tell you how you feel: Your body is numb; you are shaking. You fall on your knees and reach out, out towards the shoes. You cry, you yell and yet you cannot reach them. The wind accompanies you in your song, your song of pain. Your body has no strength left, yet you reach outward. Finally, your body gives in and your hands drop. They drop into the vast sea of shoes. You have reached them. You search desperately for those who filled them, but they are nowhere; it is hopeless. You stand and walk out leaving a piece of you behind.

Have you heard enough? Well, this is just the beginning.

Sharon Feder, 17
Vancouver, British Columbia

To Each of Them

And to each of them I will give a name and a monument
To every man, to every woman, to every child.
And to each of them I will give a name and a monument
To those who fought
And to those who had no way to fight.
To those who sang on the way to their deaths
And to those who were silent.
To those who found a God in the camps
And to those who declared God dead.
And to each of them I will give a name and a monument.
To those who went hungry so their children could eat
And to those who stole their children's bread in the night.
To those who displayed the strength of the human spirit
And to those who let the pain overtake them.
To each of them I will give a name and a monument.
To those who were there
When every bite of bread was a decision
When every step could cause more death.
To the heroes, and the non-heroes
The the strong and the weak.
To those who were superhuman
And to those who, like you and I
Were merely, most importantly
Human.

Aviva Goldberg, 17
Winnipeg, Manitoba

This Living Cemetery

Somewhere a child cries,
I hear it weep,
But it is only the wind.

I hear the whisper of footsteps,
On the cold grey stone below,
For Many
They are the concluding steps of
Existence.
They blanket the earth I walk on,
In this living cemetery –
          Majdanek

Jacob Medjuck, 16
Halifax, Nova Scotia

Forever

Walking our roads
The soil covers my skin
Crying our tears
The salt stings my eyes

Our hands shake
Our hearts sink
Our voices cry
With the memory
Of our six million

And who are they
That we hear so much about
Father, mother, brother
And I

I see you every night
A play in my dreams
With no actors
Some only know numbers
But I know faces
The frightened child
The grieving mother
The broken father

And when I awake
Your story doesn't end
You shine in the faces of every child
For you died for them

Some say you never suffered or died
I disagree
I have seen the remains of your resting place
I agree
Because forever you live inside of me

Alia Offman, 15
Halifax, Nova Scotia

We Shall Live On

The grass will talk.
The barracks will tell us.
The dust will whisper its story.

The survivors are not enough –
Their numbered arms and painful memories,
The classes, the lectures, the pictures we see – they are not enough.

Yet, the gates will speak.
And the gas chambers – they, too, can be heard.
Even the air –
      age old,
      stale,
      the key to Life itself,
Kisses our lips – so glad we are here.
Embraces our body – "stay, listen to me."
Holds our hand – knowing how we feel.

We will see.
Then we will talk.
And we will March on.
We shall live on.

Marni Beth Birnbaum, 16
Girard, Ohio

Never Again

Remembering is the key to our future,
Forgetting will destroy us as a nation,
We must never let this happen again,
Or the generations to come
Will be marching for us.

Mara Divinsky, 16
Winnipeg, Manitoba

"I would like to say Kaddish. It was always my dream to come here to see
where my parents died and whoever else died here also...
I said Kaddish not only for my parents, but for all the Jews, and all the people,
who perished here."

Peter Kleinman, Holocaust survivor
From the film *March of the Living*

Hope

After Birkenau, we toured Auschwitz, which is now one large museum. There were many blocks and each block was a memorial by a different country. By far the hardest block for me was the block of articles remaining as proof of the deaths. One room was full of shoes. One room was full of religious articles. One room was full of suitcases. One room was full of hair. The list goes on and on. The worst room for me to see was the room full of artificial limbs, braces, and crutches. My father is handicapped. He wears a brace and walks on crutches. As I looked at the display, I kept picturing him. I would see him standing there with an eery glow around him as if he were a ghost. I started to cry, and then to sob, and then I went hysterical. I will never forget the feeling that overpowered me and reduced me to nothing. It was a mixture of fear, sadness, pain, sympathy and gratitude. It made me realize how extremely lucky a person I am. I nearly collapsed in my hysterics and my friends rushed me out of the room. I didn't want to leave then. I felt I had to see this just as I had to see everything else. Yet I realize now that I did see it and staying in that room any longer could only have hurt me more.

The rest of our tour was also extremely taxing, yet once I had gotten past that one room nothing hurt me quite as much. Immediately after the tour, we prepared for our march. We lined up in rows of six (symbolizing the six million who died), held hands with our friends, and stood very close to one another. As we marched, an incredible feeling came over me. After all I had just seen, I could not believe that we had survived. I wanted to scream and shout to the world, "Hah! You thought you could kill us all but you were wrong! We survived!!!" It was a march of defiance but it was also a memorial. After my return, my mother asked me if I was dressed warmly enough. My answer was simple. We were marching remembering all the people who had marched the same route in their flimsy pajamas. What right did *we* have to complain of cold? The march was probably an emotional high for me, climaxed by the singing of *Hatikvah* at the end of our memorial. At that point, I was again in tears. Yet this time, the tears I shed were tears of victory and of hope.

As hard as it was to handle the emotional extremes on Thursday, we had a similar challenge to face on Friday. We spent the day at Majdanek – the best-preserved concentration camp. Much of it, too, was "museumified". We saw three barracks full of shoes. We saw the gas chambers and ovens. It seems terrible but I felt almost immune to everything. I had seen it all the day before and I had had my cry. I didn't shed a tear until the very end. The last two "exhibits" I saw there will remain crystal clear in my mind forever. The first was of bones. I just stared at the bones for a long time. I tried to imagine the people to whom these bones once belonged. I tried to understand the people who could watch human beings be reduced to bones day in and day out. Both these efforts, however proved impossible. There is absolutely no way that a fed, dressed, sheltered, educated, spoiled, sixteen-year-old can ever understand what happened during the Holocaust. The more I tried to, the more I realized that I would never be able to.

Continued

The second "exhibit" was a memorial. It was a huge, dome-shaped structure completely filled with ashes. They were the ashes of my people found when Majdanek was liberated. My tenth and fiftieth and one hundred and twelfth cousins were in that pile. That pile was composed of ashes of hundreds of people. People who used to be living and vibrant, doctors, lawyers, accountants... There were "Jewish mothers" and rabbis all reduced to ashes.

Never before had I heard the sound of 150 echoing sobs. 150 people stood around that pile sobbing. People I could never have pictured crying were hysterical. I could never forget that sound, nor could I forget the feeling of despair, nor could I forget the need to be supported by others while simultaneously feeling the need to support others. As I tried to recite the Mourner's *Kaddish*, and as I heard 150 other voices trying to recite the Mourner's *Kaddish*, I felt that feeling of hope rising up in me again.

Shawna Rose, 16
Toronto, Ontario

The Shadow

I am evil.
You've heard of me, of course.
I have a thousand different shapes and names,
each more hideous than the one before.
I am everywhere.
By the main gate.
Between the rows of barbed wire.
In the empty concrete chambers.
Beside the old and rusted tracks.
I am the murderer of old and young alike.
I have no conscience and no guilt.
I am evil.
And I live in the heart of man.

Aviv Gladman, 17
Toronto, Ontario

Shira Avni
Montreal, Quebec

March On

It's hard to walk on
in their shoes,
the shoes we saw
at Majdanek.
Me, without scars –
in the scraped up shoes
dirty, soft and old.
But new, for me
It's hard to decide
when to put them on –
and when to take them off.

Marni Levitt, 15
Toronto, Ontario

Siedlovic

The tiny village of Siedlovic, in the middle of nowhere, had once been quite a thriving Jewish community, until the Third Reich wiped it out. When we reached the graveyard, we were astonished to see stones chipped and cracked or fallen on their sides. Apparently, a number of them had been moved into a circle for a bonfire. There were cigarette butts ground out on Hebrew lettering. As our group stepped around these massacred memories of our people, the elementary school across the road let out for the day. Dozens of young kids, aged 6 – 8 on the average, poured out, and surrounded us, nudging each other to get better looks at the strangers. Those of us who had small badges gave them out and divided their chewing gum between the boys and girls. Then, suddenly, somehow, the children realized we were Jewish. How I don't know. Maybe it was the *Kippot* the boys were wearing. In any case, their friendly attitude changed extraordinarily quickly. They began to spit on our feet, urinated on the graves, and call out "Zhid, Zhid." A few of them stretched out their right arms and proclaimed, "Heil Hitler!"

After our initial shock, we began to move quickly back to the buses, little children tangling themselves in our feet. I resisted the urge to strike out at them, and kept my anger bottled up inside myself. Why did these children hate me? They had never seen Jews before in their short lives, and they hated us. But not just us. They hated me. Me. What did I do to deserve this kind of hate? Nothing. All I did was be myself.

When the buses had pulled back onto the road, our group leader spoke to us in Hebrew over the microphone so that our Polish guide would not be able to understand. He said that if there ever remained a doubt about the existence of anti–Semitism in Poland, we had just been given enough evidence to dispel the doubts. Into my mind popped the vision of 60 little Hitlers, standing in uniform with their right arms outstretched shouting: "Heil Hitler!" Every time I tell this story I wonder if those children in Siedlovic ever gave a second thought to their actions and as I tell myself that they couldn't have cared less, my mind reels with the implications of that statement.

Excerpted from a speech

Jessica Wyman, 17
Toronto, Ontario

Understand and remember: lest it happen again.

Haim Gorodzinsky, 18
London, Ontario

Trust

"I was asked by a Polish guard at Auschwitz for the small Israeli flag I was holding. When I asked him why he wanted the flag, all the soldier could manage to say in his broken English was "something to remember". Although I wasn't sure, he looked very sincere, and I thought he cared and understood why we were here...Anyway this is what I read in his eyes.

"I ended up giving the soldier the benefit of the doubt and I presented him with my Israeli flag. A moment later an adult chaperone reprimanded me: "Don't you know that all Poles are anti-Semites?" she yelled, "The first thing that the soldier will do when he gets home is burn the flag!" Still, when that adult advisor yelled at me, I knew in my heart that I had done the right thing. Although I'll never be sure of his reasons, I'm glad I trusted that friendly soldier and gave him my flag."

As told to Eli Rubenstein by **Chana Rothman**, 17, Toronto, Ontario

"I KNOW IT'S TERRIBLE, TRYING TO HAVE ANY FAITH...WHEN PEOPLE ARE DOING SUCH HORRIBLE THINGS. BUT YOU KNOW WHAT I SOMETIMES THINK? I THINK THE WORLD MAY BE GOING THROUGH A PHASE...IT'LL PASS, MAYBE NOT FOR HUNDREDS OF YEARS BUT SOMEDAY. I STILL BELIEVE IN SPITE OF EVERYTHING THAT PEOPLE ARE REALLY GOOD AT HEART."

From *The Diary of Anne Frank*

Stars

Stars can be many things
They can grant a wish
They can show the way
They can be a lover's tool
They twinkle happily down on us.

Stars can be many things
They can grant release
They can show millions
They can be a memory
They twinkle foreboding down on us.

Toby Fainsilber, 17
Montreal, Quebec

Cracow

I find it interesting to see how quickly the world changes. Grass grows to cover a battlefield and in Poland, the children sing songs of joy. Today I witnessed one more change. As Communism recedes and democracy is introduced, the Polish people are exercising their right to express themselves.

In the afternoon, as we walked through the old market, we saw at least 100 teenagers gathered at the centre of the market, dressed in rags, with guitars in their hands, singing songs of peace and love. This was Cracow 1990 but it could have well been Central Park, New York, 1970. It seems that the Hippie movement has finally reached Eastern Europe. There were students from Poland, East Germany, Czecho-slovakia, and they all had in common an ideal of peace, harmony and brotherhood. We decided to join the crowd singing the songs of the Beatles and other artists from the 1960's. Soon enough there were blue jackets among the tattered jeans. Hesitant at first to say we were Jews, we changed our minds as we were welcomed with open arms to sing the world's troubles and prejudices away. We sang: the Marchers and the Hippies arm in arm, brother to brother.

Can it work? During the March of the Living we debated if the Jews should forgive the Poles. Could we ever forgive the people who were involved in the Holocaust, whether directly or not? Could the world finally be ready for harmony among all its children? Singing with the Polish Hippies today I see hope in the world, but no answers...

Yoav Schreiber, 16
Montreal, Quebec

The Match

I held a shoe
only one,
not a pair.
Covered in dust
tattered and flat
the shoe maintained
only the slightest
reminder
of its occupant.
I am not certain
whether it was
a left shoe
or a right one,
but the match
was nowhere to be found.
Perhaps it lies
beneath the heap
of others like it.
Or perhaps the child
only had
that one shoe.

Joanne Raby, 17
Montreal, Quebec

THE BUTTERFLY

THE LAST, THE VERY LAST,
SO RICHLY, BRIGHTLY, DAZZLINGLY YELLOW.
PERHAPS IF THE SUN'S TEARS WOULD SING
AGAINST A WHITE STONE...

SUCH, SUCH A YELLOW
IS CARRIED LIGHTLY 'WAY UP HIGH.
IT WENT AWAY I'M SURE BECAUSE IT WISHED TO
                KISS THE WORLD GOOD-BYE.

FOR SEVEN WEEKS I'VE LIVED IN HERE,
PENNED UP INSIDE THIS GHETTO
BUT I HAVE FOUND WHAT I LOVE HERE.
THE DANDELIONS CALL TO ME
AND THE WHITE CHESTNUT BRANCHES IN THE COURT.
ONLY I NEVER SAW ANOTHER BUTTERFLY.

THAT BUTTERFLY WAS THE LAST ONE.
BUTTERFLIES DON'T LIVE IN HERE,
                IN THE GHETTO.

Pavel Freidmann
From the book I Never Saw Another Butterfly.
Written in the Theresienstadt concentration camp in 1942, its young author was later deported to Auschwitz together with 15,000 other children, of whom less than 100 survived. Pavel Friedmann died in Auschwitz on September 29, 1944.

Risen From the Ashes

It was time for the actual March of the Living. Auschwitz is really more than one camp. Auschwitz One, the area I was in, was previously a Polish military facility. Auschwitz Three, or Monowitz, was solely a slave labour camp. Auschwitz Two is also called Birkenau, and it is there that most of the gas chambers and crematoria were located. It is Birkenau that most people think of when they picture Auschwitz, with its huge watchtower entrance and its train tracks that stop right at the gas chambers, not to mention hundreds of barracks. Auschwitz II, or Birkenau, was the actual death camp. Auschwitz I is a sanitized lie about 3 kilometres from Birkenau. The March of the Living would travel the route that thousands of Jews before us traveled in order to reach their deaths in the gas chambers.

It took an hour and a half just for the group to assemble. The entire area became a virtual Tower of Babel, and as I looked around I saw the strangest things. I saw Jewish kids from around the world, from places I didn't even know Jews lived. Did you know there are Jews who live in Uruguay, South Africa, and India? They were here at Auschwitz today. I saw people from Mexico, Colombia, Argentina, Venezuela, and Brazil, not to mention Holland, Italy, Spain, Norway, Sweden, Bulgaria, Latvia, Estonia, Switzerland, U.S.A., Yugoslavia, Greece, Canada, Romania, Turkey, England, and about a thousand from Israel, who all carried Israeli flags. It was then that I realized that Auschwitz in its days of operation had been similar to this, with thousands of people in uniform (all the Marchers wore blue jackets) who spoke every language and came from dozens of countries, and they had shared only what we shared. They were all Jews, and today there was another ingathering of the diaspora behind barbed wire, but today there was a difference.

Surrounded by five thousand teenagers from around the world, I looked down at the ground I was standing on. Brown mud on a rainy day. And I realized that on every inch of brown mud where each one of us stood, a person had died, and it seemed to me as though today each person who had fallen to the earth here in blood and death had risen from the mud and ashes to join us on the March of the Living.

Excerpted

Dara Horn, 15
Short Hills, New Jersey

April Wind
(For You Who Died I Must Live On)

The April wind stirs foreign land
It scatters ashes, whispers voices of the dead
Six million lives, did perish here,
Still heard the cries of children, haunted by their fears

For you who died, I must live on
Just empty barracks, and barbed wire left to mourn
Hold out your hands, please give me strength to find your eyes,
To pray, to cry, to live to fight,
The songs you could not sing I promise I will sing

Vadim Dreyzin, 17
Winnipeg, Manitoba

Vadim Dreyzin wrote and performed April Wind *during the 1988 March. The song, from which the title of this book has been drawn, was included on an album of Holocaust songs entitled "Songs for March of the Living".* April Wind *was also used as the musical theme for a PBS documentary on the March of the Living, and on the Canadian documentary film on the 1992 March of the Living.*

I See You

I see you
I can
You give me life to see
beyond the wired gate
beyond the barracks
beyond the green fields
beyond the mound of ashes
beyond the tears
beyond the loss
beyond the pain.
You let me see the flag
waving in the wind
The freedom
to hope
The Jewish Star
I can see
But who am I to see
when you yourselves cannot.

Ron Grossman, 16
Montreal, Quebec

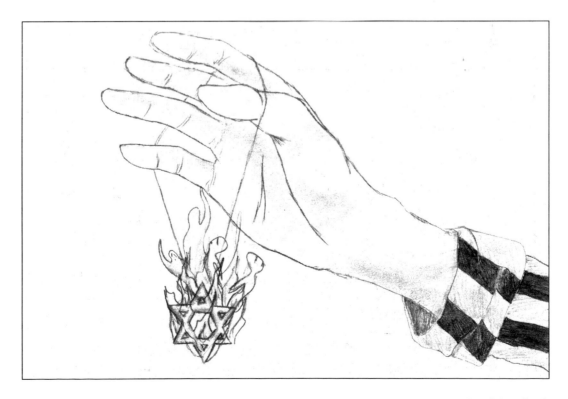

Jacob Medjuck
Halifax, Nova Scotia

The Sound of the Shofar

A shofar was blown in Auschwitz. We stood between the red barracks, thousands of people from Canada to Israel to South Africa to India, all wearing blue jackets and waving Israeli flags, and a *shofar* was blown in Auschwitz. I have never heard a more powerful sound. All of humanity might have swelled with pride at that moment. I don't know exactly what I was feeling proud of, nor exactly why my eyes were tearing. But the sound of the *shofar* in the nethermost depths of the netherworld, the presence of life in the valley of the shadow of death, was both painful and comforting, terrible and magnificent. Then, chins up, holding hands, in silence, we began to walk towards Birkenau.

Leigh Salsberg, 15
Toronto, Ontario

"**Walking out of the gates of Auschwitz was such an unbelievable feeling...
How am I so lucky? How come I get to leave, and walk out of these gates, when
so many millions never did? But a part of it was, just look at us all here, we're
leaving and we're going on to our lives, to be alive...**"

Ayelet Cohen
From the film *March of the Living*

God is Crying

Walking down the unpaved path here in Auschwitz...
thoughts fill my head I can't control.
How could God allow this to happen?
The wind howls around me,
and there are sudden changes in temperature.
The sun has come and gone within the last five
minutes, and, now, as the rain moistens my page, I am
sensing the spirits that surround me.
This rain is unlike any other rain.
These are tears.
The sky is crying.
God is crying.
Maybe God is apologizing?
Or, maybe these tears are my own?

Samantha Lomow, 17
Ottawa, Ontario

Just Outside Lublin

If hell is man's greatest fear
It is because he created it.
Two barracks full of shoes
Thousands of souls still wearing them.
Our shoes step on their graves
and we mourn
we remember
and we cry
from the bottom of our existence
for when reality had no existence
for our brothers and sisters
for friends I never knew,
but am now bonded to forever.
Cold blooded, premeditated murder.
To wipe out an entire race
for their blood,
Jewish blood.
The chosen people,
became the massacred people.
We did not count our war dead after a battle,
all we can count is the pile of ashes.
Even the smell here is of death.
In the field
the birds sing
the grass is green,
but the wind blows so cold
over the home of 800,000.
We must remember that
we are the future,
but sometimes the present
is the past.

Haim Gorodzinsky, 18
London, Ontario

Jessica Silver
Vancouver, B.C.

The Warsaw Cemetery

Domino Graves
One, Two, Three
Trees through, over, under everything
Letting nature cover their brutal deaths
Smashed epitaphs build a gate in a silent testimonial
But – it won't keep them out
A tourist attraction in green
they charge you to wash your hands
when you leave

Rana Targownik, 16
Winnipeg, Manitoba

Why?

Every minute of every day,
Every second of every minute,
Not a single moment passed
Without the question – why?

The most frustrating part of all
Is no matter how often they're asked
Nor with how much pleading
The questions remain unanswered.

Many of us looked to God
For the reassurance we craved
Only to be struck
With more queries than imaginable

My hope was somewhat rekindled
Upon our arrival in Israel,
But my confused thoughts and emotions
Remain to be reconciled.

Karyn Wasserstein, 15
Toronto, Ontario

Diary Entry: April 22, 1990

The bus ride is quiet. All eyes are glaring outside the window. Once again, a heavy fog covers the country. It is cold and damp outside, as we arrive at what seems to be Auschwitz. We stand upon the place where the greatest atrocity of all time took place. To cover their actions, the Nazis burned many documents so the exact number of those killed is not even known. It is anywhere from 1 million to 5 million. Auschwitz is not a human place, it cannot be. As we learn of the deportations from the various countries, of Jews and non–Jews, the feeling in the room is sombre. There is no talking, no crying, no laughing. Just a silence. Dead silence. No...living silence...There is one last place to visit – the gas chambers, and crematoria. We walk down a few damp and cold stairs, that same smell again as Peter, a survivor from Auschwitz, described it – it's the smell not of death, but of murder. Once again the tears began dripping; this time I wipe my face and find it wet as well. I feel like a dog, underground in a gas chamber. How can people be treated like this, killed without pity for no reason. ...We are four thousand long, four thousand strong. This will be a silent march, yet I have an urge to sing, to sing freely. We begin to march, arms locked together. As we walk along the sides of the roads, we are stared at. I cannot see the end of the blue and white sea. The colors of Israel. The colors of the *talit*. Israeli flags wave and fly in the wind. I want to sing *"Am Yisrael Chai,"* but we are silent.

Warren Levitan, 17
Montreal, Quebec

BLESSED IS THE MATCH

**BLESSED IS THE MATCH CONSUMED
IN KINDLING FLAME.
BLESSED IS THE FLAME THAT BURNS
IN THE SECRET FASTNESS OF THE HEART.
BLESSED IS THE HEART WITH STRENGTH TO STOP
ITS BEATING FOR HONOUR'S SAKE.
BLESSED IS THE MATCH CONSUMED
IN KINDLING FLAME.**

Hannah Senesh (1921–1944)
Hannah Senesh was executed by the Nazis on November 7th, 1944 after she parachuted into Hungary to join in resistance efforts aimed at helping her Jewish brethren.

i remember writing in my diary

i remember writing in my diary
in a tree outside Auschwitz
young tree, branches outstretched
and perfect to sit on
a suitable tree
for a museum;
i sat on it.
once inside, the
barbed wire behind me
i found glass
      guides
      grass in the place where some ate grass to survive;
people go on dates
to Auschwitz.
it is only now
in Canada
that i leave my room at night
and stand sobbing by a tree
my nails embedded in the bark of its trunk
branches too high to reach it is only now
that Auschwitz begins to seep through
the glass
      guides
      grass;
it seeps in torrents.

Lisa Grushcow, 15
Toronto, Ontario

A Touch of Time

I am shivering yet I am not cold.
I am crying but not hurt.
The smell of leather fills my nose,
to the point that I cannot breathe.
I reach out between the wire and touch a shoe.
It is filled with memories of death and destruction,
hard labour and the memory of a victim,
who had even his shoes stolen... how could this happen?
I DON'T UNDERSTAND.
I can only imagine the millions of people who filled these shoes,
and then had everything taken away from them, even life itself.

Another room again, another million people,
the shoes all worn, dirty and torn.
How could they take even this from these poor people?
My eyes are stinging. I can't look anymore;
my heart has fallen.
Another room. I can't take it anymore,
It's too much. How could this happen?

The floor creaks as I walk,
like the moans and groans of the people
who walked into this camp with their shoes,
but never walked out in them.
The only thing that can be heard,
is the sound of this pen on the paper,
and a few sniffles and sobbing.
But the memory is still alive and I will never forget.

Hadley Markus, 17
Edmonton, Alberta

Their Legacy

Live for today.
Cry for yesterday.
Cry for the evil
done to those
we no longer have.
Sing for yesterday.
Sing for the youths
who gave their lives
so that we
could be alive today.
Sing for those we lost,
for all the heroes,
and then,
Hope for tomorrow.
Hope that our brothers and sisters souls
will finally lie in peace
now that we are here
to carry on their LEGACY

Ariel Lustigman, 17
New York, New York

Their Crime

And then I was asked to read the names of family members who perished at the hands of the Nazis. Slowly, carefully, I recited, Yeshia, Zalmon, Moishe, David, Jacob, Chaia, Rivkah, Shandele, all the while thinking oh dear God these are the names of my mother, my uncle, my cousins, my brother, and me. Twenty-two names, twenty-two human beings dead. Their crime? They were Jewish. At that moment Poppi, I knew why I had gone to the camps.

Excerpted

Joshua Meisels, 17
North Miami Beach, Florida

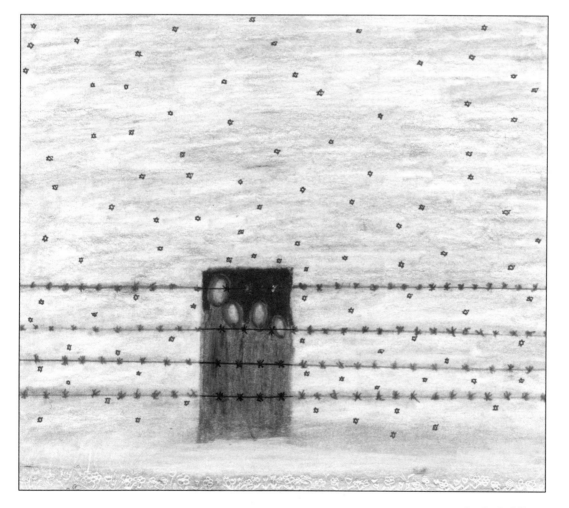

Leah Goldberg
Toronto, Ontario

A Lasting Impression

The words stop at the gates.

The camp of Majdanek was like nothing I had ever seen before. This is the camp that has been left almost untouched since the end of the war. The silence coated the camp and time stood still as I walked in disbelief from barrack to barrack. "How" and "why" were the only things that kept racing through my mind. How could a human being do this to other human beings? As I entered the third barrack, I just stood in the middle of the room, engulfed by millions of pictures.

As I walked in and out of the endless rows of barracks, I became dazed. Then came the barrack filled with shoes, and another filled right to the roof with shoes, and then another. Three full barracks with an endless number of shoes of all sizes and colours. I could smell them, that old, leathery worn-out smell. In disbelief I walked to the end of the barracks and picked up two tiny children's shoes. I held them in my hands picturing the little girl who wore them. Her image became engraved in my mind and that is what gave me the strength to move on.

From the end of the barracks we crossed through the barbed wire, down a long path to where a hugh dome of ashes stood. I sat staring into this overwhelming dome in amazement, not being able to comprehend the numbers of people who perished here. To all those people who said it never happened, I'm here to tell you it did. I felt their shoes and saw the millions of ashes.

By this time I was very upset and I had very negative feelings toward the Polish people. I saw them as mean, almost inhuman, wondering how they could ever let this happen. As I sat there deep in thought, I was approached by an old Polish lady. (A boy translated for me.) She was crying and said how happy she was to see us all here. She told me that she came here today to see us. She went on to tell of when she was a little girl and her mother hid Jewish children under their floor boards. The lady just wanted me to understand that not all people are bad. This Righteous Gentile gave me back the compassion for people that I had lost.

The ashes, as well as the rest of the camp, left a lasting impression in my mind . Above me engraved in stone was a sign above the ashes that read "Let our fate be a warning unto you." From that moment on I knew I was part of a unique chain of witnesses and I was going to make a difference.

I was going to make sure "NEVER AGAIN."

Marni Vimy, 17
Calgary, Alberta

So Wrong

I want the trees to break and fall
The grass to wither and die
I want the sky to turn black as night
The sun to go and hide

I want the air to be heavy and thick
The birds to stop singing their song
I want the stones to turn into people
To find out why humans went so wrong

Daniella Weber, 16
Vancouver, British Columbia

Rachel Kreiger
Trumbull, Connecticut

Eyes

Eyes of Nazi soldiers,
hating, cursing, crazy.
Eyes of us,
crying, hungry, praying.
Eyes of the children,
swollen and red.
Eyes of the hurting,
and those of the dead.

Eyes of the saviours
kind, refreshing, gentle.
Eyes of the victims
hollow, yearning, needing.
Eyes given freedom,
and those left in bed
Eyes of the victims with nothing left to shed.

Marni Vimy, 17
Calgary, Alberta

Jackie Abels
Miami, Florida

Shadows of the Past

She set out on a journey
    groping at the distant
    shadows
    and believing
    that she knew and understood
    their blank-dark visions
She filled herself with
    each word of the Historians
    each gesticulation of the Actors
    each statistic of the charts
She listened to her friends'
    visions –
She laughed
    their laughter
She cried
    their tears
And thought
    that they were her own
She set out on a search and now
    she was there –
    face to face with
    the shadows
    She could see –
    the blank-dark visions
    of their eyes.
And
    instead of revealing
    the answers
    She was seeking
    they let loose
    a wild confusion that
clung
    to her and
clouded
    her already hazy vision
She wanted desperately
    to flee
    to leave
    the burnt ashes
    of the past
    and return to the
        saneness
    and
        serenity
    of the present
She wanted desperately
    to feel

their pain
    to hear
    the wind's lamentations
    break the calmness
    of the stagnant nights
She wanted desperately
    to steal
    the tears
    from the heavens
    and claim them
    for her own
She wanted desperately
    to make
    sense
    of the jagged
    fragments
    of this foreign time
    and place that
She had come to know
    that had become
    a part
    of her.
But
She couldn't run away
    from her
    new-found reality
    for
    now
She knew
She knew that
    no one
    would ever
    really understand
    no one
    would ever
    really know the
        blank
        dark
        visions
    of the
        fading
        shadows
    of the
        Holocaust.

Shachy Leven, 16
Winnipeg, Manitoba

Katie Rootman
Vancouver, B.C.

Cocoons

I can't put it on paper
I
think I know so much
High and mighty
Safe in my Shaughnessy
cocoon.
Parts of me say
This could never happen.
It did
It did
I want to
slam anger onto this page,
scribble punches at it
until it spits out an answer
I want to hold this page, this
bundle of pages,
sing lyrical rhyme to it
until it sobs out an answer onto my shoulder
I want to
I want to
Write it all until
It disappears with its answer
I want to tell it
Everything will be all right
But it won't
and it wasn't
I want to
Change this, go back.
The caterpillar echoes from
My Shaughnessy cocoon.
I could have done that.
The butterfly
says
I can't do this
I want this page to
surrender
my answer.
The caterpillar knows I deserve it.
The butterfly won't hear it
And I want to slam anger onto this page
Until it yields.

Sarah Levine, 15
Vancouver, British Columbia

Shoes

Even now, months later, I can still see the shoes, thread-bare, ragged and torn. There were three rooms of shoes, rooms twelve feet high, packed from floor to ceiling with nothing but shoes. A silent memorial.

They were the shoes of those who had nothing in common and yet everything in common. They were the shoes of the young wife, who would never again know anything of play and everything about fear and survival; they were the shoes of the mother who would never sing another lullaby or hear the laughter of her children; they were the shoes of the writer, the teacher, the doctor, the dreamer.

There was a mountain of shoes reaching to forever, the shoes of a million who lived with hope, and died still believing in tomorrow. In the end, these shoes led to one place, a place with many different names: Treblinka; Auschwitz; Birkenau; Majdanek.

I remember the shoes, and I feel a deep emptiness and overwhelming sadness for what might have been. I wonder what roads might have been travelled, what words might have been written, what pains might have been eased. And I wonder what dreams might have come true.

Anita Meinbach
Miami, Florida

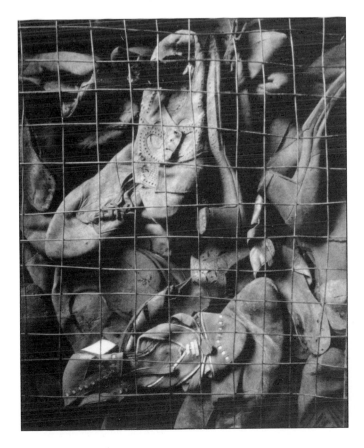

Shared Experiences

There was an amazing feeling of unity, of togetherness, of shared experiences in Poland. As we walked down the streets of Warsaw and Cracow wearing our jackets with the Star of David on them, we felt the stares and walked on. I felt pride and sadness as I walked along those streets. Sad at seeing unfamiliar things only people long dead could recognize. Proud to be walking alive and free in a city where Jews once flourished, and proud to be a Jew and proving that the Nazis did not achieve their Final Solution.

There was also a connection with the past that had not been there before. The black and white pictures in books became real life. This was not a horror movie that you pay seven dollars to see and leave two hours later. This was something you had to live with and deal with. Nothing could prepare us; all the pictures and slides and talks in the world, could not prepare us for the camps or the cemeteries, or the empty synagogues.

During the whole trip, physical gestures, a hug, an arm around the shoulders became an important way of silent communication. When the pain was too great, a hug became a transfusion of strength and comfort.

The bus was our safe haven, a buffer from whatever was going on outside, an island of normalcy where we could regain some equilibrium between one draining experience and the next.

Excerpted from a speech given at an NCSY Dinner, Vancouver, May 20, 1990.

Valerie Levitt, 15
Vancouver, British Columbia

Flowers Don't Know

Years after, it hasn't been all that long
since it happened
Some people remember the way it was
Friends and family,
now gone forever
remind us with silent screams
and pleading eyes in blank faces
Naked skeletons
now ashes
rest beneath free flying birds
and a blue sky.
Sometimes it rains
Flowers grow here
pretty and happy
They don't know what they are hiding
underneath
where it is dark and quiet
lonely

They see sunshine, and rain
birds, blades of grass
green
trees
green
now and then a person
they must think all people are sad
because they don't know
they just don't know

Miriam Naylor, 20
North Wiltshire,
Prince Edward Island

THE GARDEN

A LITTLE GARDEN,
FRAGRANT AND FULL OF ROSES.
THE PATH IS NARROW
AND A LITTLE BOY WALKS ALONG IT.

A LITTLE BOY, A SWEET BOY,
LIKE THAT GROWING BLOSSOM.
WHEN THE BLOSSOM COMES TO BLOOM,
THE LITTLE BOY WILL BE NO MORE.

Franta Bass, 1930-1944
From the book I Never Saw Another Butterfly.
Eleven year old Franta Bass was deported to Theresienstadt on December 21, 1941. She died in Auschwitz on October 28, 1944.

The Beauty Within the Beast

See the sun rise over the distant mountains
See the cloudless red glowing sky
See the soft thick grass of the rolling fields
See the endless colour in the dark green valley

Hear the birds sing playfully
Feel the warm wind cut through your hair
Listen closely to the endless silence
Smell the crisp clean country air

See the angry black clouds
Feel the cold enduring chill
Smell the dampness in the air
Hear the birds sing no more

See the endless rows of silent barracks
See the chimney spew death
Hear the voices of pain and suffering
See the face of despair

See the travesty of hatred

Ari Cherun, 16
Ottawa, Ontario

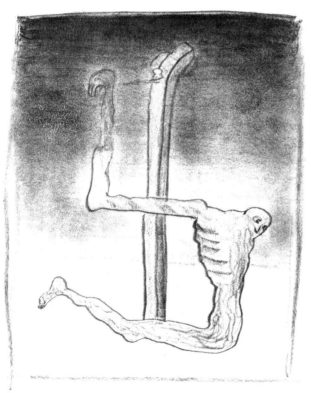

Hartley Wynberg
Toronto, Ontario

Fear

I came face to face with it, stared it right between the eyes and screamed. It was not a shark or a bear, nor the school bully... it was not an avalanche or a bomb or a bone stuck in my throat cutting the air off so I could not breathe; no, it was a plot of land with grass, trees, small buildings with bunks to sleep thirty each. It was a camp with fences of barbed wire, fearsome gas chambers and an entrance that swallowed me up. Crematoriums lined the perimeter of this death, this land, this Birkenau. This was fear for those who died and for those who lived to tell about it. I went there to see what was so scary, to understand why people were so afraid of this place. When I got there I knew why and for the first time in my small existence I saw fear. It was in the pictures on the walls of the people starved to death. It was in the barracks with a bed worn out from thirty people sleeping on it. It was in the gas chambers where two thousand people died every twenty minutes. A blanket of death lay over the camp, but the real fear, the fear I saw for the first time, was in their sunken eyes deep in the depths of their minds, long time forgotten.

Excerpted

Hadley Markus, 17
Edmonton, Alberta

The glasses really scared me.
What would I do without my glasses?
Would I be shot on the spot for being useless?

Marlo K. Shaw, 17
Toronto, Ontario

Daughter of Israel

"I am known as Lisa Melanie Jacobson. However, my Hebrew name is Shlomit Tziona. I am named after my great-grandfather and great uncle who were killed in the Holocaust. Tziona or Tzion means Israel. But I am only a daughter of Israel because 50 years ago one of my forefathers escaped the Nazis. Many other daughters of Israel before me were killed simply for being such a daughter."

This is how I began my March of the Living application essay. When I wrote those lines I had no idea that the March would become one of the most important and significant events of my life.

I cannot describe the sensation of unity I felt on the March. I know the experience changed by sense of Jewish identity. I cherish my culture more than ever and am dedicated to Israel.

...As thousands of us marched, I was reminded again of why I came; we were marching for life. In fact, our presence in Poland 45 years later was a celebration and affirmation of life. And our presence there gave Jews across the world a thousand reasons why another Holocaust would never occur.

At the beginning, one of the chaperones told me, "You're not here to cry. You're here either to be angry, to be a mourner, or to be a witness." I realize now that I was all three.

Lisa Jacobson, 16
Regina, Saskatchewan

I Wasn't There

I wasn't there
But I heard
I wasn't there
But someone like me felt
I wasn't there,
And I wish they hadn't.
I wasn't there,
But I could have been,
So easily.
I could have felt their pain,
I could have sensed their fear,
And their death –
But I wasn't there
I wasn't there and I wish they hadn't.
God, I wish they hadn't.
Why were they there?
I wasn't there.

Anonymous
Halifax, Nova Scotia
*This poem was written by a (non-Jewish) Halifax high school student, after viewing a
March of the Living presentation in her school.*

"I SEE THE WORLD GRADUALLY BEING TURNED INTO A WILDERNESS.
I HEAR THE EVER APPROACHING THUNDER, WHICH WILL DESTROY
US TOO. I CAN FEEL THE SUFFERINGS OF MILLIONS AND YET, IF I LOOK
UP INTO THE HEAVENS, I THINK THAT IT WILL ALL COME RIGHT,
THAT THIS CRUELTY TOO WILL END, AND THAT PEACE AND
TRANQUILITY WILL RETURN AGAIN."

From *The Diary of Anne Frank*

Treblinka

Today I'm a coiled spring,
Waiting,
I'm too small for my body,
Explosion.
I hold it in
In and down.
I see the trees –
The potted flowers –
I'm angry.
The pain and anger...
Not a part of me remains untouched,
The endless numbers, dates and facts.
They roll on and on – without end.
When do these horrors stop?
Ever?
What lies here?
What dreams were trapped here?
Dreams of freedom,
Dreams of hope,
In a land of nightmares.

Excerpted

Eliyanah Delicate, 16
Ottawa, Ontario

No Return

Up to a dome
which I thought would
breathe fire of eternal hope
I did not expect, once,
under me, my knees and I,
fell without support
without feeling.
I grasped the side
my head buried on, into
cold marble.
I swirled deep into the pit
tracking the years of murder
filling each ash with a face
giving each grain a name.
I arose to the rhythm of
Kaddish
my mouth in silent promise
to remember always
I climbed down from
my people
vowing not to glance back
not to give more satisfaction
not to be weak
as they would have liked.
And I know, as I knew right then
that I could never return.

Rana Targownik, 16
Winnipeg, Manitoba

Majdanek

An icy damp cave chokes the throat
The cold hurls its squeamish shrieks through the decrepit wooden infernos
A gale hurls a buckling slap to the head
The eye blinds itself to haunted shoes
And blurs at the possessed, forlorn rags
Laugh or mourn, the bleak hole of insanity gnaws in agony at the chest
The chorus of shadowed, rotted illness heaves in pain blanketing this Foreign Hell
misplaced

Jenny Lass, 17
Toronto, Ontario

My Promise

I awoke that night from the worst nightmare I have ever had. I was locked in the gas chamber at Majdanek and the gas was turned on. Those who had been with me did not realize I was missing until ten minutes later and by that time I could hardly breathe. When I was inside the gas chamber all the souls of the thousands who had died came out of the walls. They told me stories. They told me that I must live. And I did. When at last they found me I was already outside. Someone in the group had realized before all the others that I was gone and he came to find me. After that event we were inseparable. He was the only one who could come close enough to touch me and comfort me...

When I awoke I reaffirmed my promise that I would carry on their legacy.

Hadley Markus, 17
Edmonton, Alberta

"**I have never felt so alone and so helpless as I did then. I never cried so much. I felt like I should have died too – and in a way I did.**"

Perlita Ettedgui, 16
Toronto

It Has Been Noticed

All around me are graves, but I do not feel scared; I feel comforted, assured that what I'm doing is right. It is meant to stand as a message for the world. Atrocities are atrocities, no matter how many people were involved. We have come to remember. To mark it. To show–that even though somebody–many–attempted to do us in–still we have come back. We've come back to this place to show the world that harmful things cannot go unnoticed. It has been noticed and will be marked.

Eliyanah Delicate, 16
Ottawa, Ontario

Daniella Weber
Vancouver, B.C.

Realities' Deception

1. Before

stripped of every unique curve
and every birthmark depicting
life's umbilical cord of our mother's mother
stripped layer by layer until destruction
I can only imagine
the air, the smell, the ground called earth
I can only wonder of the tears and the torture
staring in the mirrors blond hair decorates my face
with two blue gems in between
a chicken pox scar embedded on the tip of my nose
I was taught to be me
I can't begin to comprehend hundreds of faces
all created from the same mold of hate
gray eyes upon rotten skin, dirt used for make-up
adding color to a walking ghost
and stories of nightmares made in heaven
as each day they awoke in hell
I pray I will never have to face an empty mirror
glass too intimidated to look back at me
g–d intended a balance of evil and benevolence
I want to stop and ask him why?
though in my heart I'm afraid of silence

2. Treblinka

lost without comprehension
I'm still breathing in a field
surrounded by birds chirping
sarcastically, mocking my thoughts
Hebrew words, sounds of comfort
in a world where I'm still crying
last words from mother to her son
the ground nurtured by nature
a bed for those passed before us
I sit on the earth,
an unwarranted grave
the soil saturated with the loss of life
a vacant field decorated with stones
and I am fortunate
I can hold your hand and remember.

3. Majdanek

from the inside, the horizon seems endless
birds echo melodies, as dogs bark
far from my walls
comprehension is a term left for those
who see through naive eyes
in search of you, I walk to understand myself
I saw your battered shoes
mounds piled to the ceiling
and your clothes
neatly hung on hangers
displayed as artifacts
your lives transformed into a museum of death
I stood where you fell, can you forgive me?
today I journey in the footsteps of victims left to ash
and tomorrow as I return to the land of the living
I face a world observing me
uniquely dressed in your worn shoes
and your stripped clothing
with my own number
JEW

4. On Leaving Majdanek

through an entangled web
I peer out at freedom
numbness encloses me,
a tight embrace,
footsteps beyond barbed wire,
the wind whips the boy's hair
as his feet entangle
with the dog's paws
ker-plop; in a chase,
they nonchalantly parade life
while I lay fathoming
how to take the next step
did your father watch my father
as I observe you now?
I'm trapped upon ashes,
buried in crimes of silence
the boy's legs carry him
racing in circles
a childhood game,
ashes ashes, we
ALL fall down

5. After

here, we are lost in another world
wrapped up in a birthday present
fastened with a bow
how reality plays with our minds
perhaps I'll never see your face again
though I walked in your footsteps
searching to understand my future
as I comprehended your past
somewhere someone in our family is crying
why are our ears closed?
I have much to gain from my outside walls
knowledge spills at my feet, calling for absorption
life becomes an open book
filled with unwritten pages
fluttering in the wind
but can you catch them?

6. You

Please remember my eyes
which never got to see a playground
and my arms which never
learned how to hang from a jungle gym
Please remember my legs
which were cheated out of learning
how to ride a bike
and my hair which I lost
as my flesh was tattooed with inferiority
Remember my hands
oh so small
with the same life line as my mother
grasping her hand in terror
as they shot my brother
Remember me because I lived and I laughed
and because I can't remember how to feel
Remember me because I could have been
YOU.

7. Realities' Deception

rain decorates my body
as g–d cries with me
the wind holds out no arms
and the sun is blinded with deception
though I'm alive,
hope smiles upside down
I saw death with my own eyes
barbed wire wrapped my heart
paralyzing my soul
what gives me the right to cry or laugh
a mirror image of selfishness
I'm one scattered in a million pieces
no one can comprehend that
until they walk through agony
breathless I am smothered under ash
pleasant dreams,
why am I the only one waking?

Sara Gorell, 16
Bridgewater, New Jersey

Diary Entry: April 28, 1992

Today is my 15th birthday. We are going to Tykocin, a town that used to have a Jewish majority (now there are no Jews living there – even those who survived the camps were chased out by their neighbors) and then to Treblinka. It will probably be one of the strangest birthdays I'll ever have.

We finally arrived in Tykocin (near Lithuania) and saw the synagogue there, which is now a museum. It is over 300 years old. It looked much like a synagogue that I had seen on one of the Greek islands, with all of its walls covered with prayer texts because not everyone had their own prayer book.

We got back on the bus and stopped at the woods nearby. Not everyone knew why we stopped there until we took our memorial candles with us. We walked into the woods on a winding path, and I took a picture of the thick canopy of trees around us. When the person next to me asked me why, I said, "Look! The forest is just like the cemetery, only without the gravestones."

The forest that *was* there *was* a cemetery without gravestones, it only had fencing around the small areas where the trees had been cleared and the Jews of the Tykocin synagogue had been shot, 1400 of them.

I write these lines for all the lines that were never written:

The trees that towered above like aloof distracted sentries
Their branches turned away from you
The blue-gray sky seeping through the leaves
(Was the sun on my face today the same sun that shone on you?)
And your patient, questioning footsteps… did you know they were your last?
I walk as you did, questioning, touching the last tree you saw
With my quaking fingers…
(were your hands as trembling as mine?)
The trees rise up overhead uncaring, each as different from the other
I stand in the clearing where, for you
The sun stopped shining
The trees stopped watching
And your footsteps ceased to question the path they took.
Yet I betray you…
I travel the return trip that you never made
As the trees around me weep hypocritical tears
That they, silent sentries, never wept for you.
I write these lines for all the lines that were never written
The beautiful day that ceased along with you.
I will plant a tree for all the trees that never guarded you
A tree whose roots will grow deep and whose branches will
reach high
A tree who will guard life and not its rival
A tree whose arms will never turn away from you.
I will remember your life instead of your death.
I will plant a tree
For you.

We leave Tykocin, making it once more "Jew-free." As we drive through more Polish farmland, I realize again that it's my birthday. This is the strangest place to be on the anniversary of the start of my life, wandering from place where graves were pre-dug for the end of other people's lives to another place where an entire complex was build for the same purpose: Treblinka.

We have come to Treblinka, and here are all the gravestones that were not in the ravine at Tykocin, or in any of the ravines throughout Europe. Treblinka, where arriving victims were met by dogs who chased them so their hearts would beat faster to make the gas chambers more effective, turned my heart into a gravestone. The camp was blown up and buried by the Nazis as they retreated.

There is only one thing left of the original camp, and that is the fire pit. In this trench, which is now filled with black stones, people who were both dead and alive were thrown into flames, and even today it smells of fire from the eternal lights which surround it. Birds sing brightly in the forests all around. I wonder if the people whose lives ended in this trench could have heard that music in their agony. I do not feel anything, I only wonder. Tears gather in my eyes, but do not leave them; they magnify the endless graveyard all around me, but like a reversed telescope, they shrink my own reactions. I stop thinking, as everyone here must have done. Outside a concentration camp, each person is different and thinks as an individual. Inside, no one thinks.

I had only brought one memorial candle, and I didn't know what to do with it. Many people were looking for certain towns and cities where they knew relatives had been murdered, but I knew of no one place that had special significance to me. I asked a friend if he had a match, but I had to light it right where I would put my candle, since the wind would otherwise blow out the flame. When I said I had nowhere to put it, he voiced my exact thought: "Then find a very small stone that everyone had forgotten, and that will be your stone." I looked around and immediately saw my stone, a tiny jagged triangle piercing its way through the ground, lost in a forest of granite. I lit my candle there and said Kaddish. I had to honor that stone, all that was left of someone else's Short Hills, someone else's Millburn, someone else's Livingston. I looked up and saw the field of thousands of people's Short Hills and Millburns one last time, and I turned to face the sun. At that moment I became fifteen years old.

As we left Treblinka, I took a handful of soil with me from beside the stones. I will bury it in Israel.

The memorial in Treblinka consists of thousands of jagged stones, some bearing names, representing many of the numerous Jewish communities wiped out by the Nazis during the Holocaust.

Dara Horn, 15
Shorts Hills, New Jersey

Thoughts of a Marcher

As I sit here and think, I notice that my hand is black with dirt. The dirt is that of a little shoe that I had been holding. The shoe is a droplet in a sea of black, encompassing my mind with its power.

The bridge beneath my feet supports me. Its stability keeps me from fully grasping the meaning of the great ocean before me. The bridge seems to protect me from the sea, so I sit down and I try to immerse myself into a frightening reality.

I pick up a shoe. It is a black boot, not quite small enough for my fingers to enclose. As I study the shoe, I try to put a face to it.

The shoe implants an image in my mind, and the image is that of a little boy. He is wearing knickers and a cap, and his smile is mischievous. He is six years old, carefree, and intrigued by the world around him. The picture that I conjure up in my mind is a happy one, but it does not correspond with my surroundings. The little boy who wore the shoe I am holding did not have many chances to play and laugh. The little boy who wore the shoe was murdered before he could work it in.

As I exit the barrack filled with shoes, I look around me at the hundreds of others. I try to image millions of faces very much like my own, who lived and died in the places where I now stand.

As I walk, I listen to the wind and I close my eyes. I feel cold. In my mind, I undress myself so that I will feel colder. I continue walking, but now I am naked, I am tired, I am weak, I am sick, I feel alone. No; I am strong, I am struggling, I have hope, I have G–d.

Try as I may, I cannot know the suffering of the Jews who perished in the Holocaust. I should be thankful that I am protected from their pain, but I cannot help but feel a flood of conflicting emotions.

I feel guilty. Yes, I am innocent of crime, but so were they. Their crime was their faith in G–d as Jews, and I carry that same faith. I walk through the camp as a visitor; I will leave Majdanek when the day is through. They never had the chance to cross the barbed wire that kept them prisoners.

I feel sad. I think of what six million could have become. I think of how much we could have grown, flourished, thrived, had we not lost our brothers... How many scholars have the Jewish people been cheated of? How much have we missed out on?

I feel angry as I stare at the mountain of ashes before me, I am in awe. The burned corpses of my kin lay a few feet from my own body. There is a lump in my throat. I am finding it hard to breathe. I see bones among the ashes; bones that once were people. But I also see bottle caps and candy wrappers. I am disgusted at the lack of respect that exists even now; even for the dead. I know that I am not in fact free, because I am still struggling for their memory and for my own existence.

I feel proud. We were not defeated. The Nazis were not successful in their mission. I, as a young Jew, can walk on the grounds of Nazi hell and light candles for the dead. We can show the world that we remember, that we will never forget the persecution that our people have endured for thousands of years... We have survived oppression, and we will continue to survive.

I feel happy. I think of Israel, the Jewish homeland. I will walk free of Majdanek, and that is luck. Next week I will walk the streets of Jerusalem, and that is not. This week we remember the Jews who died because they were Jewish; next week we'll remember the Jews who died fighting for our freedom: the soldiers of Israel.

I take my eyes away from the ashes, and around me I see thousands of youths. They are wearing blue jackets with the Star of David on their backs. It is the same star that was used to shame our brothers fifty years ago, but we wear it in pride. I realize that we are the future of the Jewish people, and I know that our fate is in our own hands. I stare at the faces who comfort each other, and I am glad to be a part of them.

As I turn and walk towards the buses, I am unsure of my emotions, for there are many. One phrase, however, is definite in my mind. It rings in my ears. It echoes, it pounds, it overrides my fears and my sorrows. My lips part and I hear myself speak,

"Am Yisrael Chai, the people of Israel live on..."

Jodi Guralnick, 17
Montreal, Quebec

"As I was marching towards Birkenau, I was carrying the flag, the Israeli flag. I felt that I was really the bearer of Jewish memory, of what happened there. I tried to think what the people, the prisoners, at these camps were feeling. Did they think that there would be Jewish people after them? I really felt the significance and the importance of us coming back, to remember them and give them the dignity they deserved. And to carry that Israeli flag affirmed for me, and maybe affirmed for them too, that this wasn't the end of the Jewish people."

Howard Liebman
From the Canadian documentary film *March of the Living*

THE LAST WISH OF MY LIFE HAS BEEN GRANTED...

...I CANNOT DESCRIBE TO YOU THE CONDITIONS IN WHICH THE JEWS OF THE GHETTO NOW LIVE. ONLY A FEW COULD POSSIBLY WITHSTAND SUCH SUFFERING. THE REST WILL DIE, SOONER OR LATER. THEIR FATE IS SEALED. FOR ALTHOUGH THOUSANDS ARE HIDING IN NOOKS AND RATHOLES, THERE IS NOT ENOUGH AIR IN THOSE PLACES TO LIGHT A CANDLE.

YOU WHO ARE OUTSIDE ARE BLESSED. PERHAPS WE SHALL YET SEE EACH OTHER BY SOME MIRACLE. THIS IS VERY, VERY DOUBTFUL. THE LAST WISH OF MY LIFE HAS BEEN GRANTED. JEWISH ARMED RESISTANCE IS A FACT. JEWISH SELF–DEFENSE AND JEWISH REVENGE ARE A REALITY. I AM HAPPY AND CONTENTED THAT I HAVE BEEN AMONG THE FIRST FIGHTERS OF THE GHETTO.

WHENCE WILL SALVATION COME?

From a letter written by 23-year-old **Mordechai Anielewicz**, *the commander of the Warsaw Ghetto Uprising, on April 23, 1943 in the middle of the revolt. It was a last call for help from the dying Ghetto to the outside world.*

Hartley Wynberg
Toronto, Ontario

HOPE

Something has embraced
and kissed this place...

From the poem *Israel*
by **Jenny Lass**, 16

Shira Avni
Montreal, Quebec

Dear Zaide:

This is a letter that I cannot send to you through normal channels. I hope you are aware of its contents.

I am your great grandson. I was born twenty-nine years after you were murdered in Auschwitz. I have just returned from a journey to that site. I walked under the words "Arbeit Macht Frei" where you walked. I sat in the barracks where you sat. I stood in the gas chamber where you stood. I touched the oven where your body was cremated.

I have since spent many sleepless nights tortured by thoughts of your pain, panic and torment, during your days in Auschwitz, the last days of your life. What did you know? Did you know of the impending doom of your wife, and many of your children and grandchildren?

As an orthodox Jewish man, you certainly knew that ours is a religion which is dependent upon love of the teachings of our forefathers. In your last days I pray that you believed that your beloved Judaism would not also die. I hope you could see the light at the end of the tunnel – that there would be a bright future – that one day, a young man who would know of you as one of his forefathers would return to the place of horror. I was there. I was there as a Jew. I was there by choice, as a free man. I was there with 3,500 other young, strong, beautiful, healthy, free Jews. I hope we represented all the Jews all over the world. Although most of the Jews are free to observe their faith, many still are not. We all know that we must dedicate ourselves to their freedom. We will never allow what happened to you to happen again.

We left Auschwitz. In a few short hours we arrived in Israel. We kissed the ground. We danced the *hora*. We thought of the six million martyrs who died. You did not die in vain. Jews have an independent homeland, in great part due to your suffering.

Zaide, though we never have met, I feel inside me, more so now than ever before. I feel you have given me so much. I keep your spirit alive by keeping your love of Judaism alive, in my love of Judaism.

Zaide, I love you.

Jason Stern, 18
Binghamton, New York

Going Back Home

I returned to the home of the entire Jewish People, the State of Israel. Coming to this spectacular country directly from Poland enhanced the experience tremendously. The transition from the death, destruction, hardship and heartache witnessed in what was once the major Jewish centre in the world, to the majesty, splendour and history of what is now our capital, was difficult to make. Many of our hearts and thoughts were still in Poland, even after landing in Israel. I also felt that I was coming here not only for myself or even for my family but for those Jews who were murdered by the Nazis without ever seeing the Promised Land. We had come home, and with us so did many others.

Excerpted

Robbie Weinberg, 16
Montreal, Quebec

Home At Last

The excitement mounted to a fevered pitch. There it was, at what seemed just an arms length away. Out the airplane window I witnessed what I'd waited to see all my life. And then they were opening the doors...

We were cheering and clapping so hard that the skin of our hands was getting sore and red. I neared the door. The excitement became so overwhelming that by the time I reached the door I could only stand in complete awe. There she was. The heat struck me in the face: I was in heaven.

I walked down the stairs of the airplane soaking in all of my surroundings. The first things I noticed were the beautiful, tall, palm trees, the flowers, the green plants and the brightest, bluest sky I'd ever seen in my life. We were hugging for joy this time. I reached the bottom of the stairs. The sign on the wall of the airport saying "Welcome March of the Living" gave an added feeling of pride, happiness and sheer relief, the relief of making it here after all the pain we'd experienced. I also felt a presence as I stood in deep thought. This time, though, it was a presence of peace, tranquility and good, the complete opposite of the evil that I felt all through Poland.

I'm in Israel. I'm home.

Karyn Wasserstein, 15
Toronto, Ontario

From my Diary: April 25

...Today we flew to Israel by Lot Air. Before we arrived in Israel, I had an empty feeling inside of me. I thought it would help if I prayed, so Mitch, Rob and I prayed in the airport in Warsaw. The feeling filled up a little bit. I think it was because I felt guilty leaving Poland. I hate the way our guide told us "This **was** a synagogue, this **was** a Jewish *shtetl*." I want him to say "This **is** a *shtetl*." I wanted to help those two Polish Jews reconstruct a community. But, now I'm in Israel. I still have feelings of guilt but I'm so happy to be here. The second I got off the plane, I kissed the ground then sang and danced with my friends. What a different atmosphere!...

Michal Cracower, 16
Ottawa, Ontario

Becky Saka
Miami, Florida

Diary Entry: May 3, 1992

We finally reached Jerusalem.

We went to the Western Wall, where the bright sun shone as though clouds did not exist, and the ancient stones towered above us. Between the giant stones were wedged millions of tiny papers, because the Wall had become "God's mailbox" – people write their secret prayers on little pieces of paper and then place them in the cracks between the rocks. I decided to drop God a line, I had some things to settle with Him… When I visited Israel before, with my family, the Wall had never been significant to me in and of itself. What made it special was that when we went there, there was always someone either laughing or crying against its side. And that didn't change. What changed was that now I was the one crying and laughing, its timeless stones watching me grow.

> **Dara Horn**, 15
> Shorts Hills, New Jersey

Israel

Something has embraced and kissed this place
Giggles tickle the honey sun which strokes life into everything
Love, and relentless, bold pride, build the stone and border
Sticky sweet greens, velour beiges, candy reds, luscious oranges, shiny prickles, crystal waters and creamy cool whites are quilted together to map out Israel.

> **Jenny Lass**, 16
> Toronto, Ontario

Jerusalem

Jerusalem.
I am here in Jerusalem.
The air tastes sweet.
The stars sparkle.
And the lights of the city grow bright!

Jerusalem.
A city which is so old,
And yet still has life
Coursing through its veins.

Jerusalem.
The city of my heart
Old and new together
They are beautiful
in HARMONY.

Eliyanah Delicate, 16
Ottawa, Ontario

Diary Entry: Arrival in Israel

We all cheered as our plane hit the runway in Israel...
We had just arrived from a country where we were unwanted and frowned upon
to a country where we were greeted with smiling faces and open arms. Watching
the young and strong Israeli soldiers made us sad that this beautiful country could
not be ours without a hard struggle. However, if we all work together, the Arab-
Israeli conflict will eventually be resolved. It will take a lot of patience and
cooperation but it can be done.

Shauna Zeilig, 15
Toronto, Ontario

In Israel

Baking hot weather,
so hot you could barely breathe,
your throat dry,
        –it didn't matter
Taking a shower, freezing cold?
        –it didn't matter

Climbing up Masada after walking in the desert exhausted,
but it didn't matter.
        Somewhere, somehow you found the strength to realize where you were and
where you just came from.
        What mattered was that you were alive, a Jew living and it became clear.
        In Israel
carrying on Judaism so vibrantly,
        being a Jew
        –it mattered

Chaya Epstein, 15
Vancouver, British Columbia

Diary Entry: May 6, 1992

Today, on *Yom Hazikaron* (Israel's memorial day), we are planting trees. Almost every tourist who comes to Israel ends up planting a tree, since it's a national project to build up the land, so I've planted trees here several time before. But this time, it meant so much more to me.

I had seen the trees in Poland, in Tykocin* and elsewhere, and it changed the way I've always looked at trees. I have always admired all trees because my mindset is that they are symbols of people. Those with the deepest roots and larger, stronger trunks can withstand the most hardship and can survive with the least water, and those with large branches and many leaves can offer the most shade to those in need. Just as there are many kinds of people, there are all different kinds of trees, while at the same time all of them seem to share a common bond in their serenity, just like I believe all people share an underlying ideal of kindness and humanity. But the kind of tree I saw in Tykocin, a red-barked fir or pine tree, now represents betrayal to me. I felt childish holding a grudge against a tree, even though it is just an outlet for my sorrow and anger, so when it was time to choose a tiny sapling to plant, I chose one that looked like the kind I had seen on my fifteenth birthday, in Tykocin.

I deepened the hole for my tree, on a hill overlooking Jerusalem, then I remembered something that I had in my backpack with me. I took out a plastic bag, and I poured its contents onto the earth around the little tree. Dark, gray-brown dirt, nearly black next to the soil that already surrounded the sapling. Mud from Auschwitz, saturated with human blood. Earth from Treblinka, gray and dusty with human ashes. Soil from Majdanek, black with human ashes and with my own tears. Dirt from Birkenau, with its weird flecks of white ashes from human bones. Out from the bag the tiny samples spilled, brushing the tree like tiny teardrops as they fell. I buried these ashes, and I used them to plant my little tree, a tree just like the ones I saw in Poland.

This was my way of remembering, of giving back something living, and I chose a tree as my gift, my own symbol of life and humanity. I'm not quite sure how long trees live, but I would like to promise everyone that this tree will live as long as a tree ever can, even when there is no longer such a thing as a tree or a person that looks away when someone cries for help. This tree will never turn away.

*See page 88

Dara Horn, 15
Short Hills, New Jersey

As The Tree Grows

A little flashlight was passed around the dark room, and every person would hold it as they spoke. Some people shared short thoughts, some told stories, some remained silent. Some people broke down as they spoke of the past, some spoke loudly and clearly of their dreams for the future. I don't know why I'd never made the connection before, but it suddenly struck me to tell the story of (my great-uncle) Joe returning to Lagow after the war and seeing a small tree growing out of the roof of the town's abandoned, damaged *shul*. We are now that tree, growing out of the destruction of the past. Some of us may be branches, some leaves. As the tree grows, some leaves may fall off, but for now, we are all a part of the tree. And we can't let anyone chop us down for firewood.

Leigh Salsberg, 15
Toronto

"THERE ARE STARS WHOSE RADIANCE IS VISIBLE ON EARTH THOUGH THEY HAVE LONG BEEN EXTINCT. THERE ARE PEOPLE WHOSE BRILLIANCE CONTINUES TO LIGHT THE WORLD THOUGH THEY ARE NO LONGER AMONG THE LIVING. THESE LIGHTS ARE PARTICULARLY BRIGHT WHEN THE NIGHT IS DARK. THEY LIGHT THE WAY FOR MANKIND."

Hannah Senesh

I Remember

I remember...

crying at the Warsaw Ghetto Memorial Service and being comforted immediately by friends, even strangers.

feeling scared as I ran alone through the Warsaw Cemetery searching for my lost March of the Living jacket.

pride as I stood before the Mila 18 Stone Memorial.

staring in wonder at the thousands of stones at Treblinka, each meant to symbolize a Jewish community destroyed during the war, with each individual community containing thousands of people.

the cold, unfriendly stares of Polish strangers.

how my faith was renewed after Nina, Amanda, and I met the young Polish man in the Warsaw Nozyck synagogue who was interested in Judaism and thought the March of the Living was a wonderful idea.

disbelief as I stood before the infamous sign Arbeit Macht Frei.

how sick I felt as I saw the Nazi swimming pool at Auschwitz and thought of Nazis swimming as Jews were dying.

laughing ironically at the thought of Zyklon-B gas being referred to on the can as "gift gas".

how my heart skipped when I saw a piece of luggage marked Irma, knowing my grandmother didn't perish here, but what if she had?

the scratch marks on the gas chamber walls and trying to shut my mind to the image of humans clawing their way to the top of the chamber where a little bit of air still remained.

placing a *Yahrzeit* candle on the railroad tracks leading to Birkenau.

smiling when my eyes caught the sight of an American flag and an Israeli flag crossed together through a hole in the barbed wire.

the beautiful *Shabbat* service in the old synagogue in Cracow.

the dissection table next to the crematoria at Majdanek.

Continued

saying *Kaddish* over the ashes and bits of bone still resting in the oven at Majdanek and forgetting the words when my feelings and thoughts took over my memory temporarily.

seeing the pits my ancestors were shot into, now covered with grass and adorned by little Israeli flags flapping in the strong wind.
the huge dome of ashes that are too heavy to be blown away.

the excitement of arriving in Israel and the "Welcome to Israel" sign at the airport.

the anger I felt when I realized that, at the *Kotel*, I couldn't pray with all of my friends, just my girlfriends.

wondering what prayer I could possibly say, as I stood in awe of the *Kotel*.

singing our songs with the soldiers at the *Kotel*.

looking in wonder at the place where David killed Goliath.

trying to bargain, unsuccessfully, for a Hebrew University t-shirt.

Sari yelling to the bus driver from her ISI trip.

tasting my first Israeli falafel.

Pam and Dana day

where I stopped when the siren sounded on Yom Hazikaron and the astonishment when I saw the birds fly over the building only after the siren had died down.

how Jewish I felt when I put on the Hebrew name necklace I'd just bought.

Josh and I dodging little kids with white foam spray on Yom Ha'atzmaut.

tasting Ben and Jerry's ice cream in Tel Aviv.

(Group 6 joining in Nine's familiar cry "Not 25".)

planting a little tree and wishing I could come back and see it grown.

getting covered with dust from the road during the truck ride through Burma Road.

playing American games with Ethiopian children.

wondering silently if I was claustrophobic as I pushed my way anxiously through the small passageways of ancient caves.

the beauty of the millions of lights, each symbolizing a child killed in the Holocaust, at the Childrens' Memorial in Yad Vashem.

climbing Masada with Jason and feeling the strain on my legs as we made our way to the top.

looking down the climbing trail of Masada, seeing the different colored glo-sticks lighting the way up the mountain.

taking six pictures of the sky as the sun rose over Masada.

seeing the Dead Sea from Masada; a still, sparkling sea like a sheet of ice that had been placed on the ground.

the huge pillow fight on the plane coming home.

how it felt to say goodbye to people with whom I'd shared an important, unforgettable part of my life, people who have seen me as no one else has.

coming home-feeling lost, separate, detached from my old life, wishing to be with group 6 again.

the rush of memories as I began to tell the story of the March of the Living to the community.

knowing I'd seen group 6 again soon: we'd already planned a reunion!

Marcela Betzer, 16
West Palm Beach, Florida

Welcome Home

The silver wings
descended from their flight
having carried me
from a place
of great darkness.
Released
from its protective clutches
I gravitated
from my carrier
towards the ground.
Images
still fresh before my eyes
of unfathomable evil
and hatefilled stares
sent chills of fear
running through my body
as sounds of screaming
rang loudly
within my ears.
At any moment
my mind could take me back
to that dreaded place
abandoned by the sun
cold and empty
filled with
nothing
but the powerful
presence of death.
But beneath my feet
now lay the warm surface
of a familiar land.
Above me,
a sheltering sky
smiled at my arrival.
A gentle wind
brushed against me
filled
with the sweet
new smells
of nature.

In its cooling breeze,
the wind lifted from my back
the weight
of a heavy burden
and set me free.
At that moment
the country had wrapped its arms
around me
like a mother,
and welcomed me –
　　　HOME.

Joanna Raby, 17
Montreal, Quebec

The Sound of the Shofar

The sound of the Shofar
is a dual one.
It is a crying, mourning, wailing sound,
It is a declaration, a proclamation, an awakening to all around.
It pierces the heart, the soul and the mind,
The message of the Shofar is dual:
One for G–d,
One for Mankind.
The Shofar was a knell
at Auschwitz
For it was being sounded at the Gates of Hell.
Six thousand Jews marched side by side,
Each representing one thousand who are but souls today:
They were the victims of an attempted genocide.
There was a message to G–d.
It was a declaration
Of thanks to the
Holy One Blessed Be He,
for fulfilling his promise to make His people
As numerous "As the sands of the sea".
And there was a message to Mankind.
Not to the Marchers, for their purpose they clearly knew,
But to the Polish soldiers and to the elderly who gazed
Upon this sight of the return of the 'ancient' Jew.
"We are Here!!" cried out the shofar
With a yearning that was infernal
"We are Here! We are not dead! We are Alive!
Yes,
We are Eternal!!!"
The Shofar was a sigh, a moan, a collectively expelled breath
at Majdanek
For it was being sounded in the Valley of Death.
People stood before a seven tonne pile of human ash, without
                    explanation and unable to find anything to say,
For their hearts were heavy and the wind blew strong,
And in Divine assent, the sky was a bleak shade of grey.
There was a message to G–d.
It was a cry of anguish
of sorrow to the
Holy One Blessed be He,
for allowing such tragedy to befall His people;
One can only stand back and say "Yes, this happened to me".

Continued

And there was a message to Mankind.
Not to the Mourners, for their purpose they need not define
But to the Polish people who kept silent then, and keep silent
                    now. It does not disturb them that Poland is 'Judenrein'.
"Remember! cried out the Shofar
All present were upset and shaken,
"Remember! Do not sleep! Do not forget!
Arise and Awaken!!!"
The Shofar was a trumpet call,
In Jerusalem
For it was being sounded at the Western Wall.
People stood before this Holiest place, also called a wall of
                    Wailing
Realizing the numbers who had died longing to stand here,
They once again found words failing.
There was a message to G–d.
It was a proclamation
of yearning to the
Holy One Blessed Be He,
That we shall soon be redeemed:
We pray and wish that "Speedily and in our days may it Be".
And there was a message to Mankind.
This one for the Marchers, for their purpose now totally clear
To tell the world of what they had seen, and "May we assemble in
                    Jerusalem next year".
"Have Hope!" cries out the shofar
Its call will always leave emotions stirred,
"Have Hope! Remember and Awaken! We are here and we are Eternal!
Fear not fellow man, the sound of the Shofar will never die!
Yes,
It shall always be heard!!!"
The sound of the Shofar
is a dual one.
it is a crying, mourning, wailing sound,
It is a declaration, a proclamation, an awakening to all around.
It pierces the heart, the soul and the mind,
The message of the Shofar is dual:
One for G–d,
One for Mankind.

Zvi Engel, 17
Montreal, Quebec

Simply Amazing

I have an amazing story to share with all of you. There was a girl on the March who came from Calgary, Canada. Her next door neighbour had a daughter who passed away in the Holocaust. Before this girl went on the March, the lady asked her to please say *Kaddish* for her daughter in the appropriate places in Poland and Israel. And this girl did. On our first full day in Jerusalem, we went to Yad Vashem, the Holocaust memorial in Jerusalem. Inside there is a children's memorial that was built about three years ago. There are five candles inside this building that are reflected off of hundreds and hundreds of mirrors, so that it seems as if there are millions of candles all around you. All else in this building is pitch black. Two recorded voices, one male and one female, alternate in the reading of some of the names and ages of the 1.5 million Jewish children who died in the Holocaust. It would take SEVEN years to complete ONE cycle of this reading! This girl from Calgary, while walking through this building for maybe 3 or 4 minutes, *heard the name of the child she had been saying* Kaddish *for!* Imagine: it would take 7 years to read through the list, and she just happened to be there for the right four minutes! Simply amazing!

Eve Pinchefsky, 15
Toronto, Ontario

One Question

We speak of two Jerusalems
One in our world
And one in the world to come
You, my brothers and sisters,
Only got to see one.
Now, as I stand before the *Kotel*
And climb Massada
Walk on the land of my two thousand year old home,
I think of you
Of where you walked
The lives you led
The lives you left behind
I've been there too
I've seen the side of my history
That isn't about
Singing and laughter and
Joy.
And I think now,
As I sit under a Jerusalem sky
Staring up at a hundred million stars
Looking for a face
In one of those windows
Is there laughter in your Jerusalem too?
Is there joy in the one Jerusalem that you did get to see?

Aviva Goldberg, 17
Winnipeg, Manitoba

Sue Klau
Miami, Florida

Israel Lives Strong

Battle builds borders
Blood sours milk and honey
Israel lives strong
Chalky crested waves
Soothe the gruff, fiery sand
Soft salty oceans
Battle builds borders
Blood sours milk and honey
Israel lives strong
Taut juicy greens sprout
Lobstered limbs and salty sweat
Till chocolaty earth
Battle builds borders
Blood sours milk and honey
Israel lives strong
Gulls slide in the sky
Dotted with white sculpted clouds
The lemon sun laughs
Battle builds borders
Blood sours milk and honey
Israel lives strong

Jenny Lass, 16
Toronto, Ontario

Finally... Home

"As I walked around Birkenau, my only sense of security (the Jews who died there didn't have this comfort), was the fact that I was carrying the Israeli flag with me. There's something so special about that flag. By carrying a Canadian flag, you show the world that you are Canadian. Similarly with the French flag, but by carrying the Israeli flag, you show the world that you are Jewish, and in a world like the one over here, where Jews are spat upon, the Israeli flag also shows the world that you are proud to be Jewish."

I carried this feeling of pride with me into Israel as I celebrated *Yom Ha'Atzmaut* amongst my Israeli friends. Although a great love for the country developed during my family's sabbatical in Jerusalem last year, it was not until after I had visited the death camps that I realized the extreme necessity and importance of the State of Israel. I felt a sense of security in knowing that all of the people around me were Jewish, that I didn't have to worry about being laughed at if I walked down the street wearing my March of the Living jacket with its *Magen David*. Finally, I had arrived home.

Jillian Moncarz, 15
Toronto, Ontario

Memories of "March"

We, all who went,
all who experienced Poland
And Israel,
Often wonder why no one cares
When we remember walking through
the streets of Warsaw,
Comparing it to the beauty
Of Israel, and wondering how
We could have possibly
Done so much and been
To so many places in
our short two weeks.
For we cannot convey the
nausea
of the horrible death camps in Poland
in contrast to the
Loveliness
Of the towers of the old city,
Looking over Jerusalem.
And we cannot discuss the meaning of
eating
Felafel
In Tel Aviv, Israel,
Our home country,
after a week of old bread, dirty radishes
and Sok
in our cemeteries.
And no one will ever, ever understand,
The happiness of...
Seeing welcome signs on stores and
hotels,
after being spat at for one week in
Poland, and after reliving the destruction
Of Six Million
And we get so angry
When our friends don't care
that while in Majdanek
One of us felt he had to stop
and hold up the group
to look once more at
The clothes of the dead,
The clothes of our grandparents.

We look at our pictures,
Each one has a story,
Each picture an aspect of
our weekstay in hell,

Our weekstay in bliss,
The whole trip a paradox in itself.
And we look through these memories,
Twenty times in a row.
With people who know
And with people who care
About our two weeks
away from our lives,
mourning and laughing,
crying and singing,
Am Yisroel Chai at Majdanek.
Still hearing Elie Wiesel singing
Eli Eli which echoed without end in
our Buses,
In our minds,
Every day of our two weeks.
Until Israel we sang,
Adon Olam without end,
To prove we were proud
To exist.
For You Who Died, I Must Live On
Became a trigger for our
tears in Poland
For our Laughter,
In Israel, when we didn't forget the dead,
Just let go of some of our pain.
Of some of our emptiness.
And we danced in Jerusalem.
Eating pita and humus.
Absorbing everything about the beauty of
Israel
Sunrise at Masada, and *Mincha* at the *Kotel*.
Independence Day on *Ben Yehuda*.
(Which we might not all remember too
clearly.)
So we must not get upset,
When our friends don't understand
Our two weeks of laughter,
pain and Happiness.
Our two weeks away from
Our lives
For to them it was only
Two weeks.

Jonny Ain, 15
Toronto, Ontario

Let's Get Serious

Funny how 50 years can last forever
But some memories not at all –
How a state founded on sweat
                    and tears
                         and pain
                              and loss
                                   and blood
             And the ashes of a near-destroyed nation,
                         Could still not be free.

Funny how in 50 years
A hatred can kill and be condemned and rise to harm again
And six million can be forgotten,
                    or worse – denied.

The world is a funny place...
                    ... Let's get serious.

Ilana Frankel, 16
Montreal, Quebec

For Just an Instant

For just an instant,
A siren is heard throughout the land.
People stop, cars stop.

For just an instant,
Opposing people with opposing beliefs
Just stop, together.

For just an instant,
He puts his gun down,
And thinks about what he's doing.

For just an instant,
They all come together as one,
Out of respect.

If they can do this
For just an instant,
Why can't they do it forever?

Alana Wexler, 16
Montreal, Quebec

On the Children's Memorial at Yad Vashem

Alone
Despite the masses
Shivering
Despite the heat
We stand, as once They did.

Stumbling
In the darkness
The paths
All end the same
Confused, as once They were.

Calling
To us softly
Voices
From beyond
We cry, as once They cried.

Years
Have passed between us
It seems
So long ago
Still, we can't forget.

Children
We all are children
Our thoughts
So much like theirs
We dream, just as They dreamed.

They,
Surrounded by darkness
And we,
Surrounded by Their light.

Ayelet Cohen, 16
Montreal, Quebec

Yad Vashem is the site of Israel's national Holocaust memorial in Jerusalem.

Israel... for me was like coming up for air while swimming. I had been in one of the deepest darkest places of humanity – drowning. Knowing that Israel was my "oxygen" supply enabled me to continue. This feeling "crescendoed," and by the time I was on the runway at Ben Gurion, I had surfaced... Although Israel helped heal my spiritual and emotional wounds... at home in Vancouver I would find that I have a scar, a scar that will be with me forever...

Tali Hyman, 16
Vancouver

Reflections

Reflections of the cold wind seeping through the evil cracks
The barracks full of emptiness, cold, and helplessness
The stench of stale leather
Shoes upon shoes upon shoes

Reflections of the hate, the bitterness, the tears
The numbers
Millions upon millions
The silent cries of the children
The figures envisaged in the ashes that soon disappear with the wind

Reflections of the questions and the pain
The grasping for something that is out of reach

Then our home, our holy land
The beauty reflecting the darkness
The incredible love reflecting the bitter hate
The future reflecting the past
The smiles reflecting the tears

Now my home
It is surrounded by mirrors

Marni Segal, 16
Vancouver, British Columbia

Whispers of Remembrance

I close my eyes and feel the
warmth of the sun, but I can't
close my ears to the cries of pain.
And I will never close my mind to
the whispers of remembrance.

Dana Bookman, 17
Toronto, Ontario

Home

Thoughts–
jumbled and confused
Heart–
heavy and full
Answers–
distant
Time–
unknown
Still–
purpose and duty must prevail!

Lauren Otto, 17
Hamilton, Ontario

ELI

O LORD MY GOD,
I PRAY THAT THESE THINGS NEVER END:
THE SAND AND THE SEA,
THE RUSH OF THE WATERS,
THE CRASH OF THE HEAVENS,
THE PRAYER OF THE HEART.

Hannah Senesh

Epilogue

Over the Atlantic, May 12, 1993

The following is an excerpt from a letter written by Anna Heilman to 40 Canadian university students who accompanied her on her first trip back to Poland since the end of World War II. Anna Heilman, a survivor of the Warsaw Ghetto Uprising, and the death camps of Majdanek and Auschwitz, helped smuggle gunpowder into Auschwitz-Birkenau which was used in the destruction of Crematorium No.3 by the Jewish Sonderkommando in the camp. The Nazis executed hundreds for this act, including four women, one of whom was Ester Wajcblum, Anna's sister. The women were hanged on January 5, 1945, less than two weeks before the camp was abandoned by the Nazis. The four women are honored at Yad Vashem (Israel's national Holocaust memorial) and a plaque at Auschwitz recognizing their role in the uprising is also being planned.

❖   ❖   ❖

We are on the plane from Paris to Warsaw. In Warsaw a big bus with rickety air conditioning awaits us and we go directly to Majdanek. I feel dingy and uncomfortable. I didn't brush my teeth. I start to cry, hoping nobody sees me. The day after Ester's execution I got up to brush my teeth and I suddenly realized that the world will go on without her, and it won't make any difference to anybody. It was then that I lost my mind and my friend and fellow prisoner Marta took over. (Marta saved my life on numerous occasions, both during the execution of my sister Ester and her three unfortunate collaborators in Auschwitz on January 5, 1945, for their acts of sabotage in Auschwitz, and soon after, on January 18, 1945, when the Germans decided to evacuate Auschwitz and took us on their infamous death march. I had lost my mind and refused to budge, but Marta physically dragged me along with her.)

We went back to Majdanek on a glorious May spring day, I mean in 1993. The chestnut trees are in full bloom and the fruit orchards cover the earth with a pink canopy. The checkered fields are a picture of rich brown earth and green sprouting wheat. From time to time we can see farmers plowing their fields with a horse-drawn plow. Flocks of birds descend on the fields picking up the seeds. On the road we pass families and farmers on horse-drawn carts. From inside the bus the scene is pastoral. We arrive at Majdanek. Nothing looks the same, yet everything looks familiar.

I don't see the gruesome camp displays in front of us. I am reaching back in memory. Where were we? This block? That block? This camp, that camp? Does the guide know the story? Yes he does. He seems to care, he is credible.

I only talk when my memories differ with his narrative, when I am reaching in and ask him to verify my memories. *Yes they seem to be accurate.* And I talk, when the students ask me, their questions probing, sensitive, bring back memories and associations not lost but deeply buried...until we come to the collective grave of the ashes, a round mound of ashes that were carefully scooped to rest in one place under a protective dome of grey stone that looks like a Kippa on the reassuring head of a father.

And I talk here, and a student asks me. *"How do you feel"?* If he would not ask me I would not have put my feelings into words. And what I felt there was relief. I have found my parents' grave. Finally. I can, at last, recite a prayer at their place of rest.

And now, sitting on the plane, on my way home, I don't remember what I told the students, but I suddenly feel that it was not me talking, that I was surrounded by thousands of faces, smiling at me, pushing me, talking to the students through my voice, saying: *"Tell them, tell them and thank them for us, for coming here, for remembering us and for never forgetting."*

Hanka (my Polish name)

Anna Heilman,
Warsaw, Poland/Ottawa, Ontario

… I would like
to promise everyone
that this tree will live
as long as a tree ever can,
even when there is no longer
such a thing as a tree
or a person that looks away
when someone cries for help.
This
tree
will never turn away.